WINDOWS 95
in easy steps

GW00690829

Harshad Kotecha

COMPUTER
STEP

In easy steps is an imprint of Computer Step
Southfield Road . Southam
Warwickshire CV33 OFB . England

Tel: 01926 817999 Fax: 01926 817005
http://www.computerstep.com

Reprinted 1998, 1997, 1996

Notice of Liability
Every effort has been made to ensure that this book contains accurate
and current information. However, Computer Step and the author shall
not be liable for any loss or damage suffered by readers as a result of
any information contained herein.

Trademarks
Microsoft® and Windows® are registered trademarks of Microsoft
Corporation. All other trademarks are acknowledged as belonging to
their respective companies.

Printed and bound in the United Kingdom

ISBN 1-874029-28-8

Contents

First Steps

This chapter shows you how to start and shut down Windows 95. You'll also learn how to use the Start button and the extensive on-line help.

Covers

Introduction

Microsoft Windows 95 is a major upgrade of all the following operating systems used on personal computers:

- MS-DOS
- Microsoft Windows 3.1
- Microsoft Windows for Workgroups 3.11

Windows 95 brings together features available in older-style operating systems and adds to them so that you can do more work quicker from your desktop or portable computer. Some of the main benefits include:

- Improved interface

- Easier file management, including support for networked connections and long filenames

- New Plug and Play feature automatically detects and uses additional devices you attach to your computer

- True 32-bit multitasking enables several programs to run simultaneously so you can get more work done

- Improved search facility

- Better multimedia support

- Extended communications capability, including E-mail, faxes, bulletin boards, Internet.

The basic foundation underlying Windows is its 'windowing' capability. A window (spelt with a lower-case w) is a rectangular area used to display information or to run a program. Several windows can be opened at the same time to work with multiple applications, so you should be able to dramatically increase your productivity when using your computer.

Using a Mouse

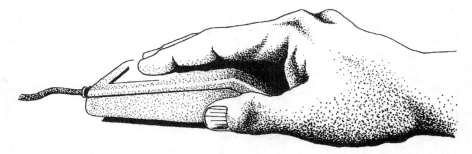

A mouse is a pointing device used to communicate with your computer. It is recommended that you use Microsoft, or Microsoft-compatible mouse with *Windows 95*.

To use it, first place it on a flat surface or use a mouse mat. You will notice an arrow-headed pointer ( ) moving on your screen as you move the mouse.

To make a selection, move the mouse pointer on top of an item and then press and release (or click) the left mouse button. Sometimes you can click twice in rapid succession to select an item (double-click).

A mouse will usually have at least one more button on the right (called the right mouse button). This provides further facilities - for example, a right-click of the mouse button when it is over an appropriate object will display a shortcut menu of related options for further selection.

A mouse can also be used to move items on the screen. This is achieved by first moving the mouse pointer over an item. Then, press and hold down the left mouse button and move the mouse to position the item. Finally, once you see the item in the new location, release the mouse button. This technique is called 'dragging'.

In this guide we will use the terms: Click, Double-click, Right-click and Drag to refer to mouse operations described above.

Starting Windows 95

After you switch on your computer you will be asked to log on to Windows, or to the network if your computer is linked to others.

If you don't want to use a password, click OK without typing one in, the first time you log on. This window will then not appear in future.

Then the Welcome window is displayed on the desktop:

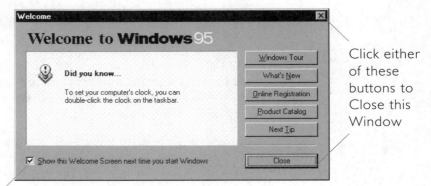

Click either of these buttons to Close this Window

Click here if you don't want to see this window each time you start Windows.

The Welcome window is useful, especially for a beginner. Click on the Windows Tour button and follow the instructions on screen to get a basic 'feel' of the features available in Windows 95. Click on other buttons, as required. Note that Online Registration is only available if you have a Modem connected to your computer.

The Desktop

The new desktop is less cluttered than in previous versions. You should only have a few *icons* from which all tasks can be performed easily. As a result, most of the desktop is a tidy blank area.

 Your desktop may look different, depending on components you have installed and any customisation that has been done.

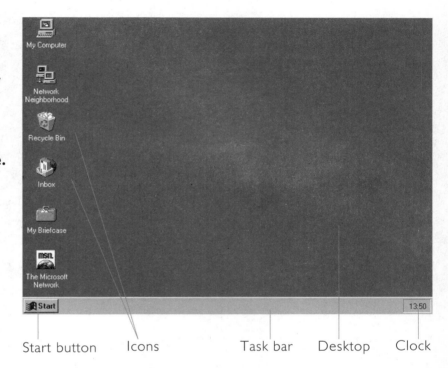

Start button   Icons   Task bar   Desktop   Clock

Double-click on any icon to launch a major facility available in Windows 95 - you can create your own shortcut icons for frequent programs that you'll be using.

Only a single click is required on the Start button to access and run all your programs, change settings and use the Help system.

The Taskbar at the bottom can be moved to any of the other three edges of the desktop. A Task button is created on here automatically for every program running - click on it to switch between them.

The Start button

The Start button on the Task bar is designed with the beginner in mind. Because it is *not* intuitive for a beginner to double-click the mouse button to launch a program, the Start button allows you to select and start a program quickly just with a single mouse click. Other common tasks that you need to do using your computer are also available directly from the Start button.

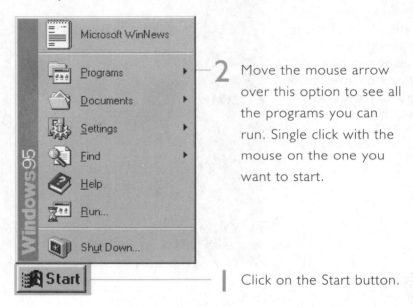

2 Move the mouse arrow over this option to see all the programs you can run. Single click with the mouse on the one you want to start.

Click on the Start button.

The Start button options include:

Programs	Quickly allows you to start a program
Documents	Enables you to start work on one of the 15 most recent documents you've been working on
Settings	Allows changes to settings for your computer
Find	A sophisticated search facility
Help	A complete on-line Help system
Run	Used to start a program
Shutdown	A safe way to switch off, restart or log off your computer.

On-Line Help

The Help system in Windows 95 has been completely re-designed and improved. Choose Help either from the Start button, or from the Menu on some of the windows.

HANDY TIP

Higher level help is available from the Contents tab, or specific word-based help from Find.

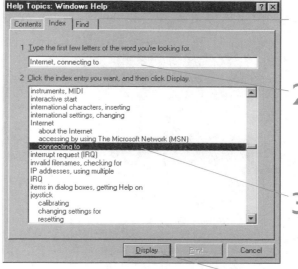

Click on the Index tab if not selected.

2 Type as many letters of the word you want help on.

3 Click on the appropriate matching word.

HANDY TIP

Click on green underlined text for its definition.

REMEMBER

Help Topics takes you back to the main Help selection screen. Back displays the previous window.

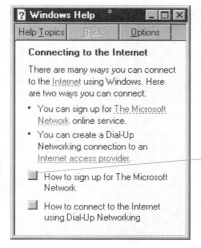

4 Click to display an outline help window for the topic chosen.

5 Click on a button for further specific help.

Shortcut button

Some Help windows will contain a Shortcut button. Clicking on the Shortcut button will directly display the actual referenced window. For example, if you are getting help on how to change your computer's date, you can change it there and then as you are reading about it.

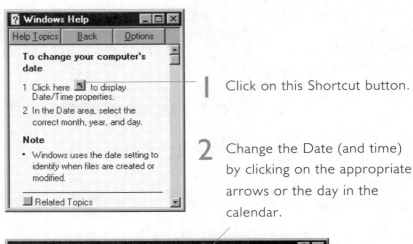

1 Click on this Shortcut button.

2 Change the Date (and time) by clicking on the appropriate arrows or the day in the calendar.

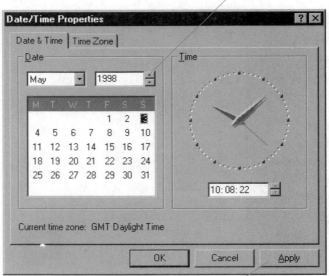

3 Click to confirm the new date/time, or click on OK to achieve the same and close this window.

? button

Many windows will have a [?] button. Use this to display an explanation of any object on the screen.

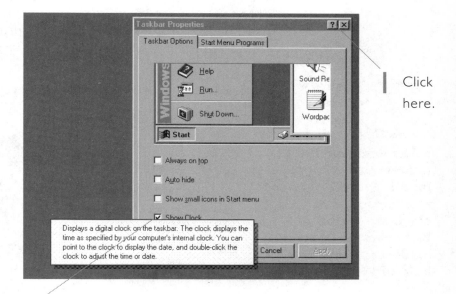

Click here.

2 With your mouse pointer changed to ▷? click on any object in the same window for an explanation of it.

3 Click anywhere to close the explanation box.

Wizards

If you have been using Microsoft Word or Microsoft Excel applications, you will already be familiar with Wizards. These guide you through a series of questions and enable you to complete a complicated task. The best way to illustrate the way Wizards work is with an example. Assume that you wanted to install a printer to work with your computer:

HANDY TIP

Wizards can be used to install other devices, like a modem or fax, or to install a new application. Even the Installation of Windows 95 itself is made easy with the help of Wizards.

| Select Printers either from the Settings option available from the Start button, or from the Control Panel window.

2 Double-click on the Add Printer icon to install a new printer.

3 Follow the instructions given in a series of boxes.

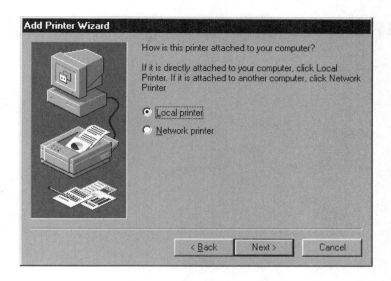

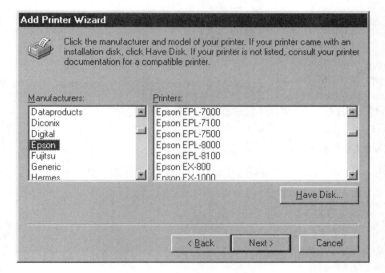

4 Click on the Back button to change options from the previous box, or Cancel to abandon the procedure alltogether. Otherwise, continue to select Next until the last box which replaces this button with Finish.

Shutting down your computer and Windows 95

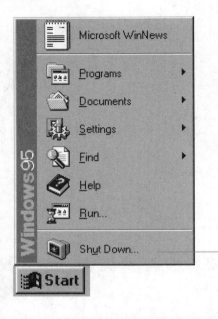

| Click on the Start button, and then on Shut Down...

Only switch off when the message, "It's now safe to turn off your computer." is displayed on your screen.

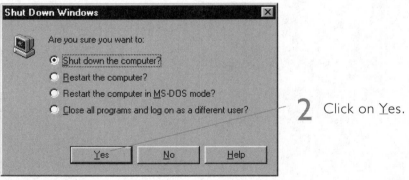

2 Click on Yes.

You may not need to switch off your computer if you're using a newer system with Power management – it will be done automatically for you.

Normally, you'll leave the default first option selected and click on the Yes button. A message, "Please wait while your computer shuts down", is then displayed. This is when Windows checks if any changes to your documents are saved and prompts you if they're not. It saves its own settings and closes all the files properly.

Basic Controls

Everything you do in Windows 95 will be done using a menu, dialog box or a window. This chapter shows you how you can use these structures.

Chapter Two

Covers

Menus

Many of the windows will have a Menu bar near the top, displaying the menu options relevant to a particular window. Simply click on a menu option to reveal a drop-down list of further options within it. As an example, we will look at the View menu from the My Computer window:

A tick shows that an option is active.

A bullet also shows an option to be active but only one option can be selected from a group. Clicking another option from the group will automatically turn off the previously selected one.

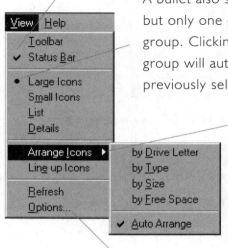

A forward arrow indicates that there is another linked menu for selection. Move the mouse arrow on the option to see it.

The ellipse (i.e. ...) indicates that if this option is selected, an associated window with further selections will be displayed.

To deactivate an option with a tick next to it, click on it. Click on it again to activate it.

If an option is dimmed out, it cannot be used at that particular time or is not appropriate.

Some options may have shortcut keys next to them so you can use these instead of clicking on them with your mouse.

Dialog boxes

Although simple settings can be made quickly from menu options, other settings need to be made from windows displayed specifically for this purpose. These are called dialog boxes.

Tabs - click on the appropriate one to display its settings.

Check boxes - click on as many as required. A tick indicates that an option is active - if you click on it again it will be turned off. If an option is dimmed out, it cannot be selected.

Radio buttons - only one out of a group of radio buttons can be selected - if you click on another radio button, the previously selected one is automatically turned off.

Action buttons - **OK** will save the settings selected and close the dialog box or window. **Cancel** will close the window without saving the amended settings - click on it if you've made a mistake. **Apply** will save the settings selected so far but will not close the window, in case you want to make further changes.

Structure of a window

All windows are similar in their structure. You can have a window containing icons for further selection, or a window that displays a screen from a program.

Dialog boxes are usually fixed size windows and therefore don't have scroll bars, minimise, maximise, restore buttons or the control icon. They also don't display resize pointers at the edges.

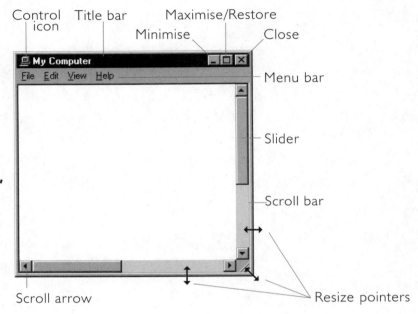

Control icon   Title bar   Maximise/Restore
                    Minimise   Close

My Computer

File Edit View Help

Menu bar

Slider

Scroll bar

Scroll arrow   Resize pointers

Double-click on an icon to open a window relating to it.

From the View menu, click on Toolbar to display further buttons under the menu bar, or click on the Status Bar option to display a bar under the bottom scroll bar - this displays information about items selected from the window.

The scroll bars will only appear when there are items that cannot fit into the current size of the window.

If you move the mouse pointer over any edge of a window, the pointer changes shape and becomes a double-headed resize pointer - drag it to change the size of a window (see page 26 - Resizing a window).

Moving a window

As long as a window is not maximised occupying the whole screen, you can move it. This is especially useful if you have several windows open and need to organise your desktop.

 REMEMBER **You can also move a window by clicking on the control icon (top left) and then using the four directional cursor arrow keys on the keyboard to move in any direction.**

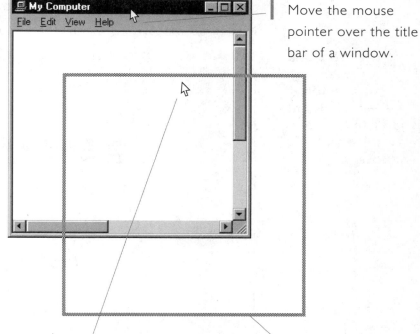

Move the mouse pointer over the title bar of a window.

HANDY TIP **If you have installed Microsoft Plus, you can have the Full window drag feature so that the whole window moves as you drag the mouse, instead of just the frame.**

2 Drag the mouse pointer to a new location.

3 When the window frame is in the desired location, release the mouse button.

Maximising, Minimising and Restoring a window

A window can be maximised to fill the whole screen, minimised to a button on the Taskbar, or restored to the original size.

You can also double-click on the Title bar to maximise the window.

Maximised window   Minimise button   Restore button

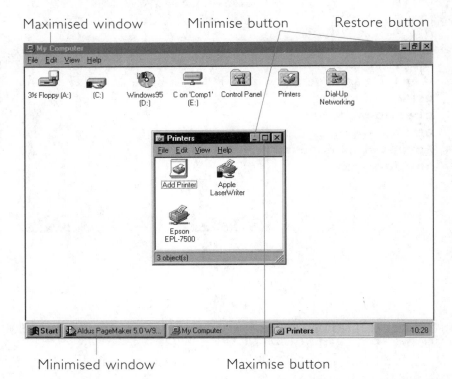

Minimised window   Maximise button

Click the Control icon (top left) or right-click the Task button to display a shortcut menu that also allows you to minimise, maximise and restore the window.

Whether a window is maximised or original size, click on the minimise button (left of the top-right three buttons) to reduce the window to only a Task button on the Task bar. This will create space on the desktop for you to work on other windows. When you want to restore the reduced window, simply click on it from the Task bar.

The middle button (out of the three) can either be a maximise button, or if the window is already maximised the same button changes to a restore button.

Switching between windows

Switching between windows cannot be easier. The task (window) that is active always has its Title bar highlighted. If you have more than one window displayed on the desktop, click anywhere inside a window that is not active to activate it or switch to it.

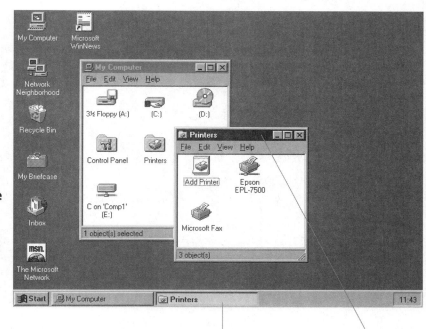

active task button   active window

If you have too many windows open, Task buttons will resize themselves automatically.

Press the Alt+Tab keys to toggle and switch between tasks.

Another method of 'task switching' is to use the Task bar at the bottom. Every window that is open has a button created automatically on the Task bar. Therefore, it does not matter if the window you want to switch to is overlayed with others and you cannot see it. Just click on the button for it in the Task bar and the window will appear on top and it will be active.

Resizing a window

As long as a window is not maximised or minimised, it can be resized.

 HANDY TIP **Resize and move windows on your desktop to the way you prefer to work.**

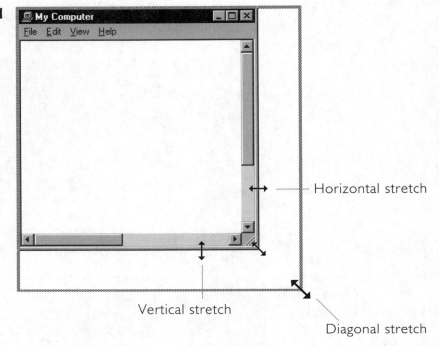

Horizontal stretch

Vertical stretch

Diagonal stretch

| Place the mouse arrow anywhere on the edge of a window (including corners) - it will change to a double-headed resize pointer.

2 Drag the pointer outwards to increase the size of the window, or inwards to reduce the size.

3 When the outline is in the correct position, release the mouse button - the window will now occupy the area previously shown by the outline.

Arranging windows

If you have several windows open on your desktop and want to automatically rearrange them neatly, rather than resize and move each one individually, use the cascade or tile options from the Toolbar.

To avoid cluttering your desktop, try not to use the Cascade and Tile options - it is better to use the Minimize All Windows option so if need to work on any one, it is only a mouse-click away from the Task bar.

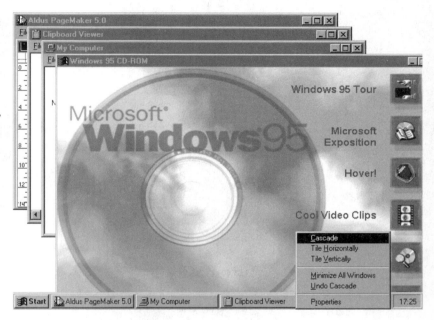

Click on Undo Tile to restore your own arrangement of windows before you tiled them.

1 Right-click on the Task bar to display a shortcut menu.

2 Click on Cascade (overlaps all the windows so that just the Title bars are visible, except for the front one), Tile Horizontally (resizes each window equally and displays them across the screen in rows), or Tile Vertically (resizes each window equally and displays them across the screen in columns).

Arranging icons

If you have icons displayed (large or small) in a window, you can rearrange the order, either manually or automatically.

Manually

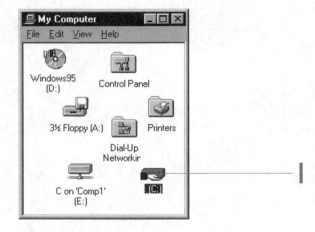

Drag an icon to any space within a window.

Automatically

HANDY TIP

You can drag an icon out of the window and onto the desktop or another window.

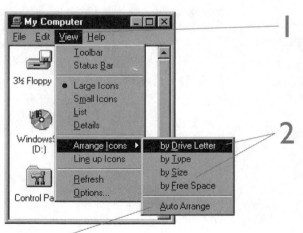

Click on the <u>V</u>iew menu, and move pointer over Arrange <u>I</u>cons.

2 Click on an option to neatly arrange all the icons in a preferred sequence.

3 Click on <u>A</u>uto Arrange to activate it with a tick, so that if you resize the window, the icons are rearranged automatically.

Scrolling

If a window is not big enough to display all the information within it, then Scroll bars will appear automatically - either vertical, horizontal, or both. Use these to see the contents of a window not immediately in view.

The size of the Slider in relation to the Scroll bar indicates how much of the total contents are in view. The position tells you which portion is in view.

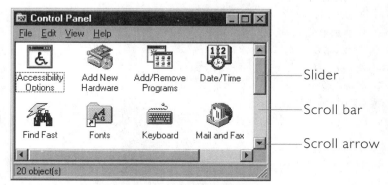

Slider

Scroll bar

Scroll arrow

1 | Drag the Slider along the Scroll bar towards one of the two Scroll arrows to scroll in that direction.

or

2 | Click on the Scroll bar to scroll just a little towards the Scroll arrow nearest to it.

or

3 | Click on one of the Scroll arrows to scroll just a little in that direction. Hold down your mouse button to scroll continuously.

Closing a window

When you have finished with a window you will need to close it. There are many ways of doing this - use the method you find the easiest.

 Save your work before closing a program window that contains work you've been doing.

 Click on the Close button (top right corner).

If Minimised

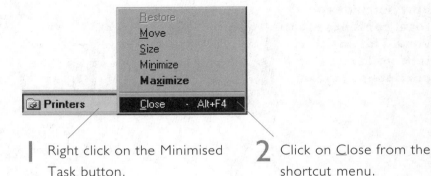

I Right click on the Minimised Task button.

2 Click on Close from the shortcut menu.

From the Control icon

I Click on the Control icon (top left corner).

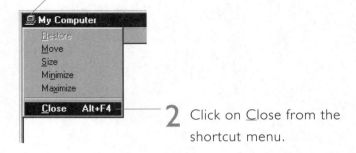

2 Click on Close from the shortcut menu.

From the keyboard

I Press Alt-F4 keys to close the active window.

Working with Programs

Most of the time you'll be using your computer to run a program or an application you have installed. Find out how to start programs and how Windows 95 can help you organise them for fast easy access.

Chapter Three

Covers

Starting and Closing Programs

The Start button enables you to quickly start any program listed under the Programs option. When you first upgrade from a previous version of Windows, all the Program Manager entries are automatically listed under this Programs option. You can add new programs to this list, or remove entries for programs not used very frequently (shown later in this chapter).

HANDY TIP

If you are using a Program frequently, drag its icon onto the Start button and it will appear at the top of the Start menu for an even quicker start to that program.

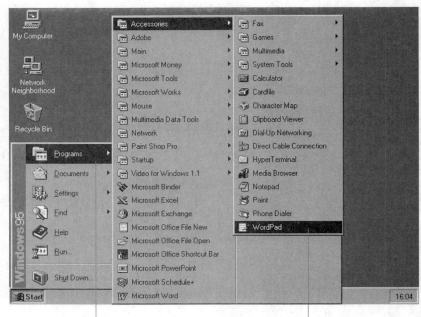

HANDY TIP

Double-clicking on a program icon from the desktop or a window starts the program too.

1 Click on Start and move the mouse pointer over the Programs option.

2 Click on a Program name you want to start. A name with a forward-arrow is a program group rather than an actual program. Move the pointer over it to display a cascaded menu of programs that are under it.

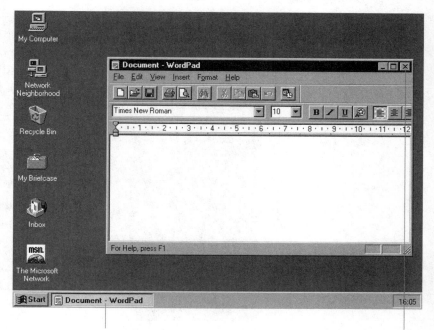

3 A button for the program appears on the task bar and the program starts in its own window.

4 Click on the Close button or click on Exit under the File menu to quit the program.

Starting a Program using Run

The Run command from the older version of Windows is still available in Windows 95. It is usually used to run the setup program to install a new program, from say the A: floppy disk drive or the D: CD-ROM drive. However, you can use the Run command to start any other program already installed in your computer.

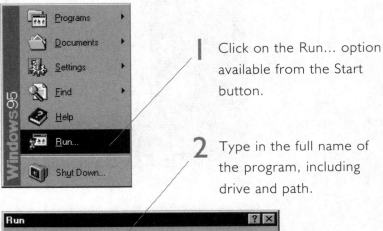

Click on the Run... option available from the Start button.

2 Type in the full name of the program, including drive and path.

Click on the pull-down arrow to see previous commands used. Then click on one of these commands (if appropriate) instead of typing it in.

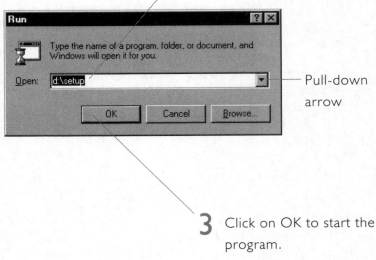

Pull-down arrow

Browse... allows you to find the program and insert the path and name in the Open box.

3 Click on OK to start the program.

Creating a Shortcut

A *Shortcut* can provide easy access to a program you use very frequently. You can place a shortcut on the desktop or in a folder.

Shortcuts can also be created to access other objects, including documents, folders, disk drives, printers, modem, fax and even other computers.

 REMEMBER

If you delete a shortcut, the file that it relates to is not deleted and if you delete the file, the shortcut is not automatically deleted.

1 Drag an item onto the desktop using your right mouse button.

2 Release the mouse button to display a small menu next to the item.

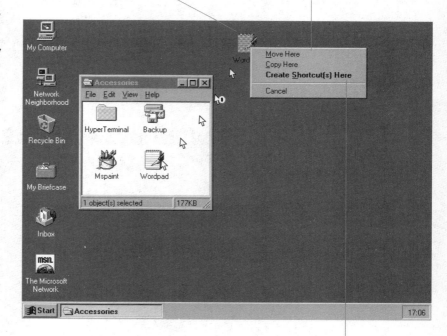

3 Click on the **Create Shortcut(s) Here** option. The shortcut will then appear. Note that the shortcut icon is different from the original because it has a small shortcut-arrow at the base.

Adding Start Menu Programs

The Programs menu displayed from the Start button can be changed to enter new programs or delete old entries that are no longer required. Changes you make here do not affect the actual programs stored on disk - these entries just allow you to start the programs quickly!

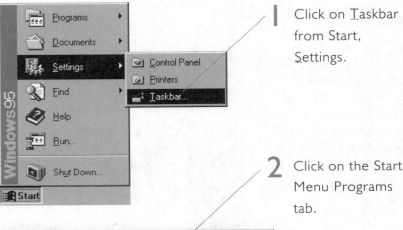

1 Click on Taskbar from Start, Settings.

2 Click on the Start Menu Programs tab.

HANDY TIP **Click on the Remove... button instead of the Add... button to delete an entry from the Start Programs menu.**

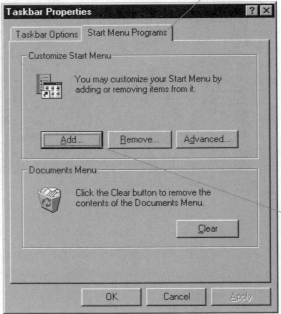

3 Click on the Add... button.

...cont'd

 HANDY TIP **Click on the Browse... button if you don't know where the program is stored.**

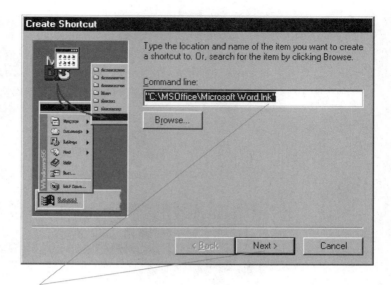

4 Type in the full name and path of the program in the Command line box and click on the Next> button.

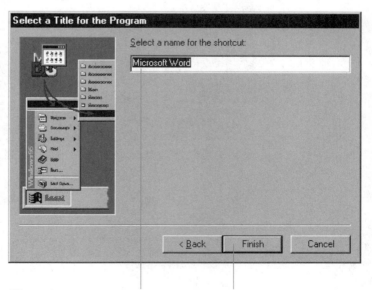

5 Type in a meaningful name for the program as you want it to appear on the Start Programs menu. Click on Finish.

Using the Startup Folder

As with the previous version of Windows, the Startup feature is also available in Windows 95. This allows a program or several programs to start automatically after the computer is switched on and Windows has started. Therefore, you can start work straight away on a program that you always use.

| Click on Windows Explorer available from the Start button, Programs.

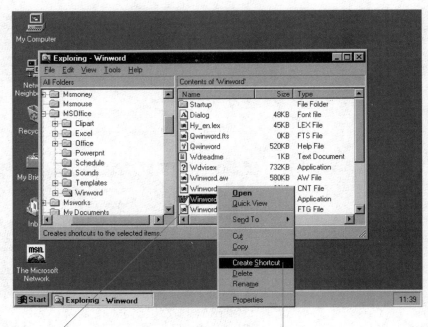

2 Find the program you want by clicking on it using your right mouse button.

3 From the small menu displayed, click on Create Shortcut. A shortcut icon of the program selected is created.

...cont'd

You can use this technique to move any program to any folder.

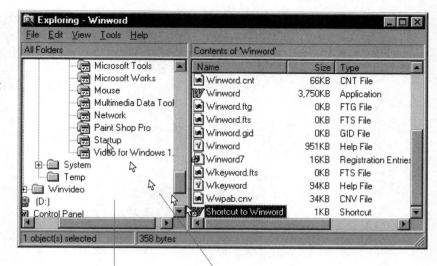

4 From the left column of folders, find the Startup folder. To find it you may need to click on the plus sign next to the Windows folder to expand the hierarchy of folders under it, then the Start menu, and then the Programs folder. The Startup folder should be in this last Programs folder.

5 Drag the shortcut icon created onto the Startup folder. The program it relates to will now start automatically each time you start Windows.

Starting Programs Minimised

Sometimes you may want to start a program but not have it take over most of the desktop. You therefore need to set it up so that when it's started it is minimised automatically. When you are ready to use the program you will then only need to click on its button on the taskbar.

1 Click on the Start button with your right mouse button and click on Open from the shortcut menu displayed.

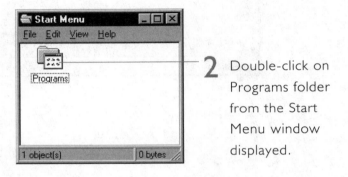

2 Double-click on Programs folder from the Start Menu window displayed.

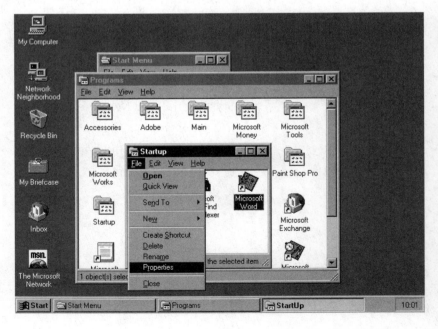

...cont'd

3 Double-click on the Startup folder from the Programs window and click once on the Program in the Startup folder you want to remain minimised when started.

HANDY TIP

You can also select Properties by clicking on the right mouse button after the Program is selected.

4 Click on File and then Properties from the menu.

5 Click on the Shortcut tab.

Microsoft Word Properties ? ✕

General | Shortcut |

Microsoft Word

Target type: Application

Target location: Winword

Target: `C:\MSOffice\Winword\WINWORD.EXE`

Start in:

Shortcut key: None

Run: Minimized ▼
        Normal window
        Minimized
        Maximized

Find Target...   Change Icon...

OK   Cancel   Apply

HANDY TIP

You may want several programs to start automatically when Windows starts. It is best to have them minimised, as in this example, so you can easily access them as you need to from the Task bar.

6 Click on Minimised after clicking on the pull-down-arrow.

7 Click on OK.

Install and Uninstall Programs

You can add (Install) new programs or just the uninstalled components of an existing program. You can also remove (Uninstall) a program - this feature is similar to that povided by the special Uninstaller utilities on the market. Note that Windows 95 can only uninstall programs specifically developed to use this new feature in this version.

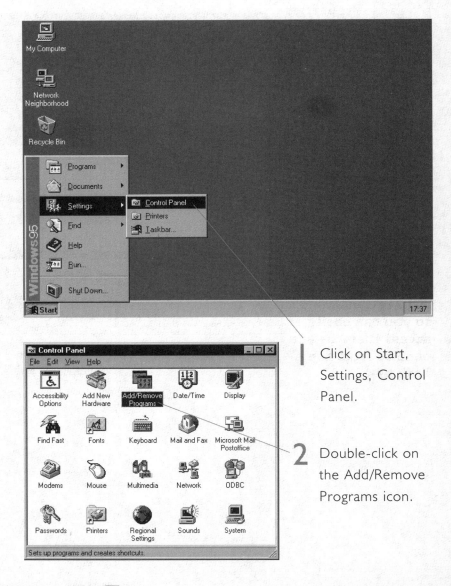

Click on Start, Settings, Control Panel.

Double-click on the Add/Remove Programs icon.

...cont'd

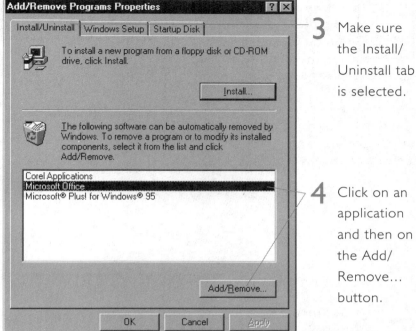

3 Make sure the Install/ Uninstall tab is selected.

You'll need to have your software disks or CD ready before you can continue.

4 Click on an application and then on the Add/ Remove... button.

HANDY TIP

Compare the disk space requirement to the total space you have to determine how much of the software you can afford to install.

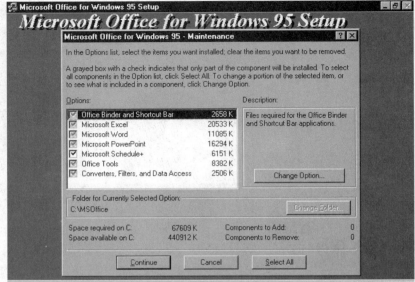

REMEMBER

A tinted tick box ☑ indicates that some components of the program are installed. A clear tick box ☑ indicates that a program or component is fully installed. Click on these little boxes to control exactly which components are added/removed.

5 Follow the instructions on screen to add/remove software components.

Cut, Copy and Paste

You can move or copy information (text, graphics, etc.) from one Windows program to another, or within the same program, through a temporary storage area called the clipboard.

 You can also use Cut, Copy, Paste from the Edit menu.

 Press the Print Screen key on your keyboard to copy your screen display to the clipboard.

| Start a Program, say Paint, and select an area.

2 Right-click the mouse button and select Copy from the menu displayed to copy the selection to the clipboard (Cut is same but it deletes the selection too).

 If you cut or copy another object , the previous one will be lost. Switching off has the same effect. You can save the contents of the clipboard by choosing the Clipboard Viewer program from Accessories.

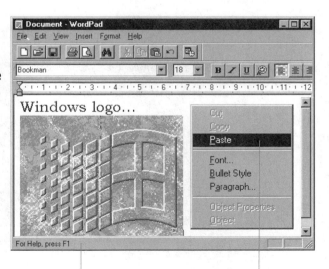

3 Start another program, say WordPad.

4 Right-click the mouse and select Paste to copy the clipboard here.

Saving your Work

Whichever program you work with, at some stage you will need to save your work (letter, spreadsheet, drawing, etc.) as a file. There are two types of saves: changes to an existing file (Save), and saving a new file created for the first time (Save As).

REMEMBER

Just click on Save to save the changes to an existing named file.

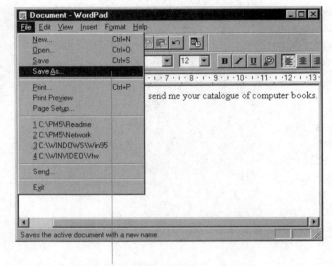

From the File menu, click on Save As.

HANDY TIP

Use Save As to copy a file by giving it another name/location.

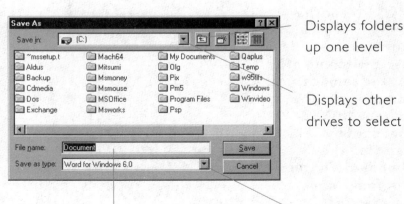

Displays folders up one level

Displays other drives to select

2 Type in a name here for your new file and click on the Save button.

Displays other file types you can save in

Running MS-DOS Applications

You can still run older MS-DOS programs (including games) in Windows 95. In fact, there is better control for MS-DOS through Windows 95; like variable-size window and scroll bars, copy and paste between Windows applications, different size TrueType fonts, etc...

1 From the Start button, select Programs and then MS-DOS Prompt. The MS-DOS Prompt window displayed is like any other window, including title bar, contol buttons (minimise, maximise, close), scroll bars, resize capability. Even the task button is created and you can work with MS-DOS and Windows applications at the same time.

Font/size   Mark   Copy   Paste   Full-screen   Close

HANDY TIP

Press Alt+Enter to make the MS-DOS Prompt window full- screen if it is windowed, or vice versa.

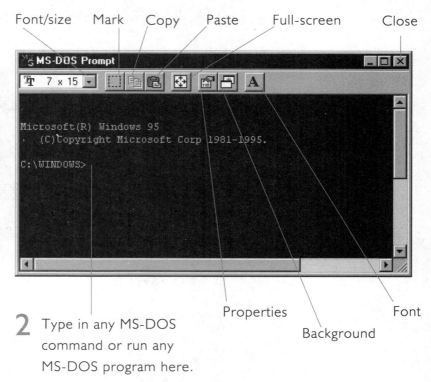

Properties   Font
Background

2 Type in any MS-DOS command or run any MS-DOS program here.

3 Click on the Close button or type Exit to close the MS-DOS Prompt window.

Using the Old Program Manager

If you were very comfortable with the old Program Manager window in version 3.1 and 3.11, you can still see it and use it until you get used to the new, improved interface in Windows 95.

Click on the <u>R</u>un... option available from the Start button and type PROGMAN in the <u>O</u>pen box, then click OK.

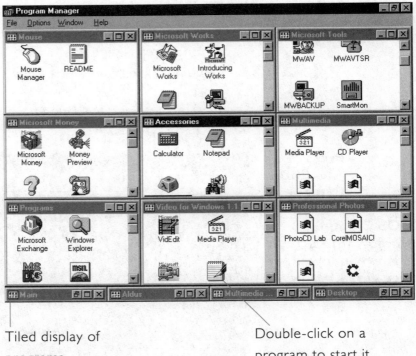

Tiled display of programs

Double-click on a program to start it.

Looking at Files

A file is the most basic unit of storage in Windows. All your work on the computer is stored as files and so are all the programs you use.

There are various ways of browsing/accessing files and the folders that contain them.

Chapter Four

Covers

My Computer

One way to look for all your files, regardless of where they are stored, is to double-click My Computer, usually located on the top left corner of the desktop.

My Computer

Double-click this icon.

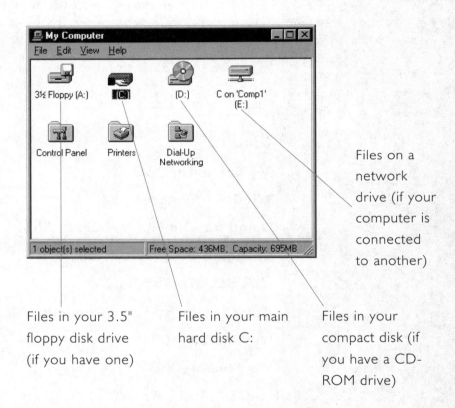

Files on a network drive (if your computer is connected to another)

Files in your 3.5" floppy disk drive (if you have one)

Files in your main hard disk C:

Files in your compact disk (if you have a CD-ROM drive)

2 Double-click on the appropriate drive icon from My Computer window.

...cont'd

A file is a basic unit of storage. All your programs and documents are stored as files.

Folder

File

A Folder is same as the older term, directory.

3 Double-click on a folder to display files it contains or other folders.

You'll notice that a standard Windows file icon is used if the file is not associated with a specific application. Examples of files that are associated with applications and therefore have their unique icons to identify them include:

Word

Excel

Paint

Windows Explorer

Another way to look at your files is to use Windows Explorer. This is equivalent to using File Manager in the previous version.

Starting Windows Explorer

HANDY TIP

Right-click on the Start button and click on Explore for a faster start.

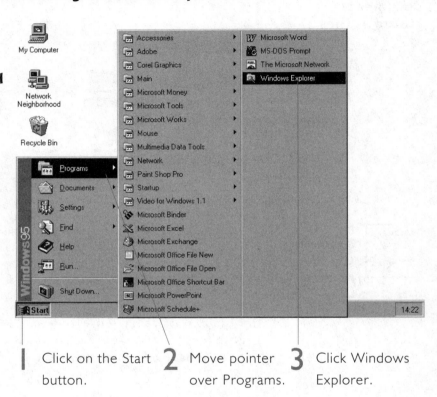

| Click on the Start button. **2** Move pointer over Programs. **3** Click Windows Explorer.

Other ways of starting Windows Explorer

HANDY TIP

Also right-click on other icons from the desktop, or a folder, to start Explorer showing contents of the item chosen.

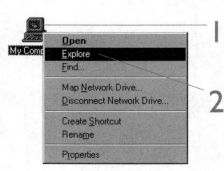

| Right-click the My Computer icon on the desktop.

2 Click on Explore from the shortcut menu displayed.

...cont'd

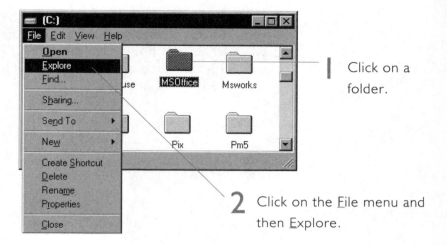

Click on a folder.

2 Click on the File menu and then Explore.

Windows Explorer display

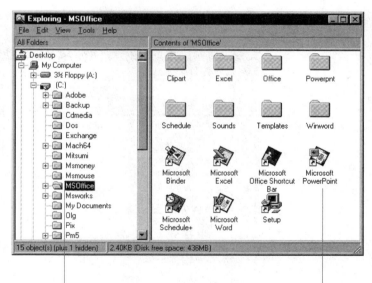

Click on a folder you want to see the contents of. Folders and files it contains are displayed on the right side.

2 Double-click a program icon to start it, or a document/folder icon to open it.

The main benefit of using Windows Explorer instead of My Computer is that it displays a structured hierarchy of all your drives and folders on the left. Click on a plus sign next to a folder to see other folders it contains, and on a minus sign to hide this detail.

Expand folder

Collapse folder

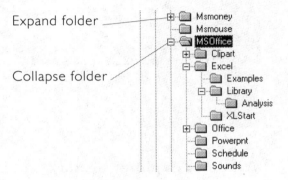

Altering the split between panes

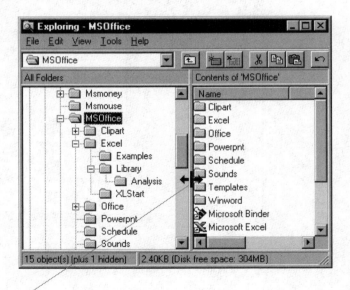

1 Move the mouse pointer over the border so that it becomes double-headed.

2 Drag the border towards left or right, as appropriate.

Using the Old File Manager

If you are very familiar with the old File Manager window in version 3.1 and 3.11, you can still see it and use it until you feel more comfortable with Windows Explorer.

Click on the Run... option available from the Start button and type WINFILE in the Open box, then click OK.

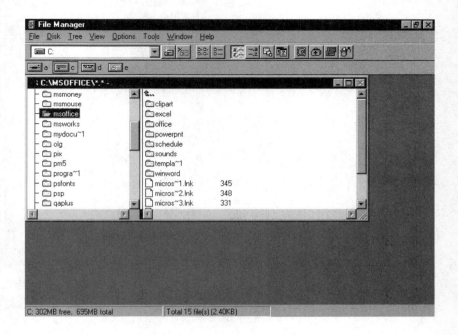

Changing the Display

Whether you are using Windows Explorer or displaying files using My Computer, you can change the display of files by using the View menu.

1 Click on the <u>V</u>iew menu option.

2 Click on one of the display options.

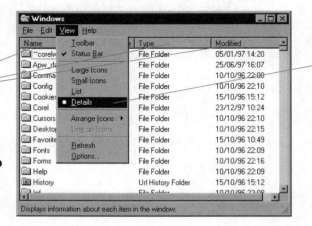

Details shows the size of file, type, and when it was last modified.

HANDY TIP

Click on any column heading to sort the list by that field, or click on it again to sort it in reverse order.

Using the Toolbar

REMEMBER

The same Toolbar buttons are available from Windows Explorer and My Computer.

The Toolbar provides buttons that make it easy to manage your files/folders.

1 Click on Toolbar from the View menu so that it is activated and ticked.

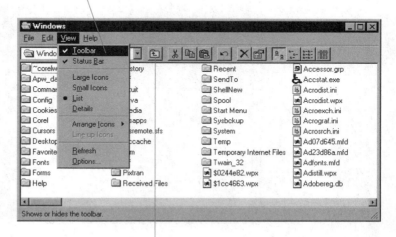

2 Click on the Up One Level button to display the previous folder.

HANDY TIP

If you want to see a folder at a higher level but don't want to bother with the Toolbar, just press the Backspace key.

      Go one level up to a higher folder

      Connect and disconnect to a network drive

      Cut, Copy and Paste a file or a folder

      Undo last operation

      Delete and Display properties of a file/folder

      Change the display of files/folders

If you move your mouse pointer near the bottom edge of a button and hold it there for a few seconds it will tell you what the button is for to remind you before you click on it.

Browsing with a single window

When using My Computer, sometimes you will need to open several folders before you reach the one that contains the file you need. Each folder you double-click on opens a window and soon your desktop will be cluttered with windows you don't need.

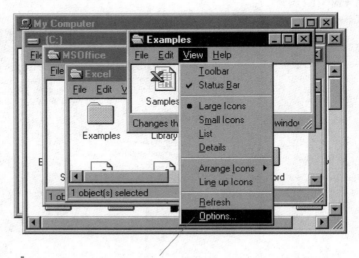

Click on the <u>V</u>iew menu and then <u>O</u>ptions...

The default, separate window for each folder is useful if you need to move or copy files between the open folders.

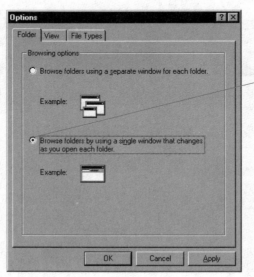

2 From the Folder tab, click on Browse... using a single window.

Quick View

This is a new feature that allows you to look at a document without opening it or starting the program that created it. You don't even have to have the program associated with the document installed!

BEWARE

Quick View has to be installed as an accessory in Windows 95, and can't be used for documents created using uncommon or new-version (post-Windows 95) programs.

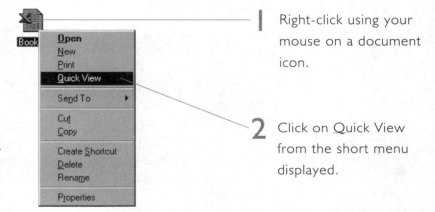

1 Right-click using your mouse on a document icon.

2 Click on Quick View from the short menu displayed.

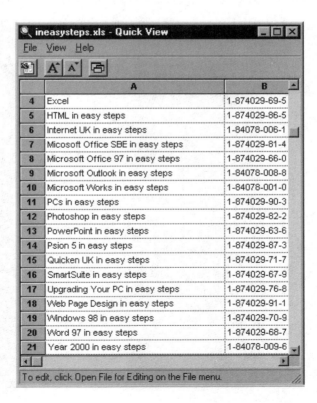

File Naming

Up until Windows 95, long filenames such as those on Apple Macintosh, have not been possible on the PC. Now you can have a filename of up to 255 characters. Therefore you can be more descriptive when naming your files instead of being confined to just 8 characters, and 3 for the file type or extension.

Example of a long filename

When you rename a file, the hidden extension remains unchanged.

Although the file extension is now not normally displayed, it's still used to maintain backward compatibility with the older 16-bit applications and MS-DOS. To display the file extension:

From any folder, click on Options... from the View menu.

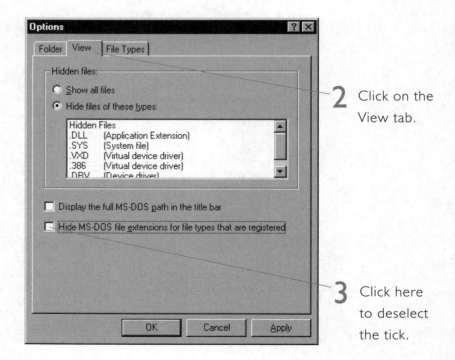

2 Click on the View tab.

3 Click here to deselect the tick.

Hidden Files

You will not normally see all the files that exist in your computer. The reason - some are deliberately hidden from view in case you accidently change them or delete them. These important files usually help Windows and other applications/devices to work properly. They are best left hidden. However, if you need to view them:

From any folder, click on Options... from the View menu.

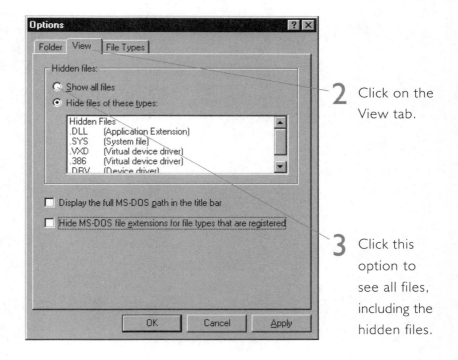

2 Click on the View tab.

3 Click this option to see all files, including the hidden files.

Opening Documents

Windows 95 offers several ways of opening your documents and the programs that created them without having to first start the program and then to open the document from within the program.

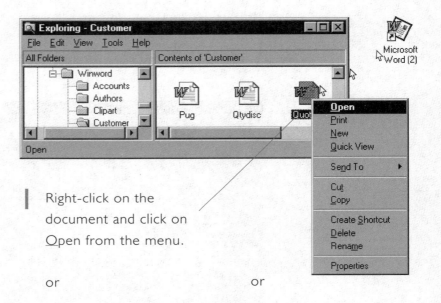

1 Right-click on the document and click on Open from the menu.

or

2 Select the document by clicking on it once and choose Open from the File menu at the top.

or

3 Just double-click on the document icon.

or

4 Drag the document icon onto the Program icon, either on the desktop or a folder.

or

5 Drag the document icon over the Task button for the Program; don't release the mouse button. When the Program window opens, release the icon.

Working on Recent Documents

Quite often you'll want to open a document you have been working on recently. Windows stores the 15 most recent documents you have been using under Documents from the Start button, to give you fast access to them.

HANDY TIP **You can clear the display of these documents by selecting Settings, Taskbar..., Start Menu Programs tab, and clicking on the Clear button.**

Click on the required document from this list.

File Properties

Every item - file, program, shortcut, device - has Properties. You can access the Properties dialog box for all in the same way. The purpose is two-fold:

- to display basic information about the item

- to change settings for the item

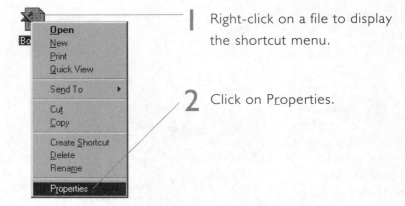

1 Right-click on a file to display the shortcut menu.

2 Click on Properties.

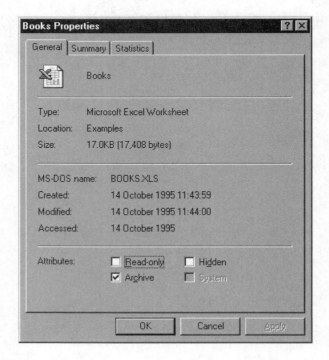

Chapter Five

Managing Files and Folders

Remember that Folders are just logical names where files are stored. Windows handles operations on Files and Folders (like moving, copying, deleting, etc) in a similar way and so they are both covered together here.

Covers

Selecting Multiple Files/Folders

To select a single file or folder you know that you just click on it once to highlight it. Then you can move, copy or delete it (see the next topic). However, if you want to perform these operations on several files or folders you'll need to select all of them, so that they can then be manipulated efficiently, in one fell swoop.

Adjacent block of files

 To de-select all files, click once anywhere outside the selection area.

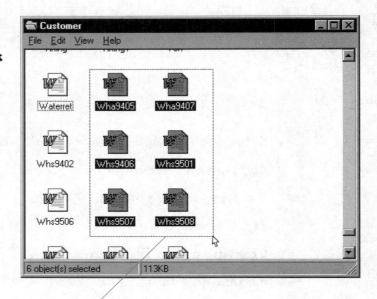

 Selecting files here can include whole folders, which may contain other files.

1 Drag out a box to cover all the files you want selected.

or

2 Click on the first file and then press and hold down the Shift key. Then click on the last file. The whole block of adjacent files are selected.

Non-adjacent files

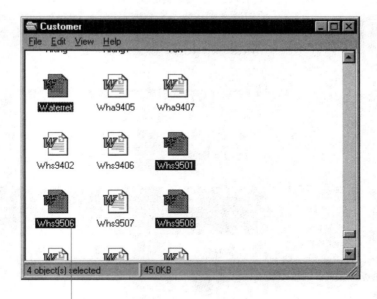

To de-select a file, Ctrl+click on it again.

To select several non-adjacent files, press and hold down the Ctrl key. Then click on as many files as required.

To select all files (and folders) in a window, click on Select All from the Edit menu.

Copying and Moving Files/Folders

You may want to copy/move a file to the same disk
(different folder) or to another disk (e.g. floppy disk). There
are several ways you can achieve this. For speed and
simplicity, however, the first method, using the right
mouse button is recommended.

Using the right mouse button

Start Windows Explorer and select the folder that contains
the file you want to copy or move.

**Instead of
a single
file you
can copy/
move multiple files
(just select as
shown in the last
topic), or copy/
move a folder using
the same technique.**

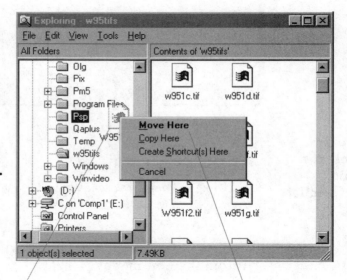

2 Using the right mouse
button drag the file you
want to copy/move onto
the destination folder or
drive so that it is
highlighted. Then release
to display a shortcut
menu.

3 Click on Move Here or
Copy Here option.

...cont'd

Using the left mouse button

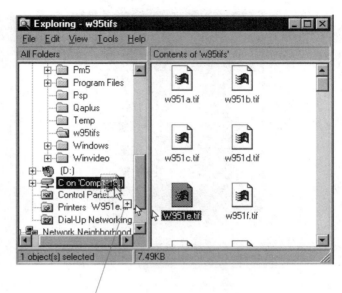

| Using the left mouse button drag a file (or multiple files/folders) to the destination folder or drive.

2 To move/copy files to the same drive or to another drive, follow this simple technique:

Copy to another drive   **just drag**
Move to another drive   **press the Shift key when dragging**
Copy to same drive   **press the Ctrl key when dragging**
Move to same drive   **just drag**

You'll notice a little '+' symbol in a box if the file is going to be copied. Otherwise, the file will be moved.

Using Cut, Copy, Paste

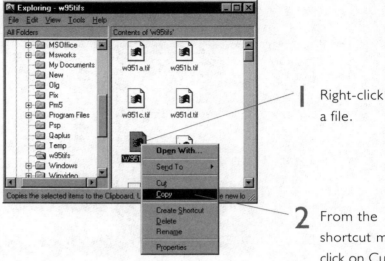

1 Right-click on a file.

2 From the shortcut menu click on Cut (to move) or Copy.

3 Open a window for the folder you want to copy/move the file into. Then right-click the mouse button in a blank area of the window.

 You can also use Cut, Copy and Paste from the Edit menu.

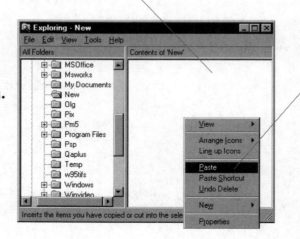

4 Click on Paste from the shortcut menu.

...cont'd

Explicitly to a Floppy disk

Make sure there is a floppy disk in your drive before copying or moving files to it.

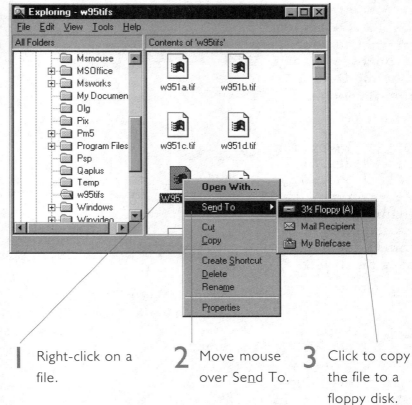

Keep the Shift key pressed when selecting the floppy disk to Move the file instead of Copying it.

1 Right-click on a file.

2 Move mouse over Send To.

3 Click to copy the file to a floppy disk.

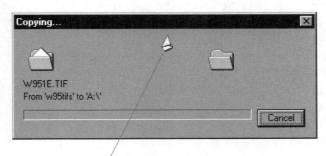

An animation of a file flying across is shown whenever a file (or group of files) is moved, copied or deleted.

Deleting Files/Folders

You can press the Delete key on your keyboard instead of selecting Delete from the menu.

This is easy and safer (see next topic, Recycle Bin too). Note that you can delete a file from wherever it is listed, although My Computer display is shown here.

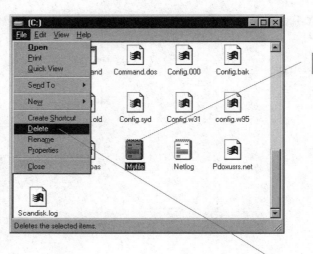

Select a file/ folder by clicking on it, or select multiple files (see earlier topic).

Delete can also be chosen by right-clicking on the file and selecting it from the shortcut menu displayed.

2 Click on Delete from the File menu.

A message to confirm deletion and to send the file to the Recycle Bin is then displayed. Confirm by clicking on the Yes button.

You can also delete a file by dragging it onto the Recycle Bin icon on the desktop.

If you suddenly realise that you have made a mistake deleting a file (or several files), choose Undo Delete from the Edit menu straight away. Alternatively, use the Recycle Bin to retrieve it (see next topic).

If the Shift key is pressed down when deleting a file/ folder it will be deleted permanently rather than going into the Recycle Bin.

The Recycle Bin

BEWARE

Files that you delete from your floppy disk or from the MS-DOS command prompt don't go into the Recycle Bin.

The Recycle Bin is a place where deleted files are kept. They are not physically deleted from your hard disk until you 'empty' the Recycle Bin. The Recycle Bin therefore provides a safety net for files you may delete by mistake and it allows you to easily retrieve them.

A drawback of the Recycle Bin is that from time to time, you'll have to empty it to free up disk space taken up by deleted files.

Recycle Bin

| Double-click on the Recycle Bin icon from the desktop.

HANDY TIP

To make it easier to find the file, you can display this list by Name, Origin, Delete Date, Type or Size. These options are all available from the View menu, Arrange Icons.

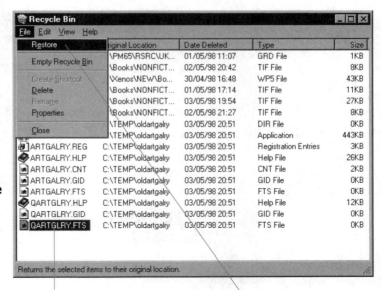

2 Click on a file you want to restore, or multiple files with Ctrl-click (Shift-click) as described earlier.

3 Click on Restore from the File menu to rescue the file back to its original location (or choose Empty Recycle Bin to reclaim lost disk space).

Creating a New File/Folder

You can create new files in standard formats for use with specific programs installed on your computer. Also using the same option, you can create new folders to organise your files into.

HANDY TIP

The New option to create a file/folder is also accessible from the desktop. Just right-click the mouse button.

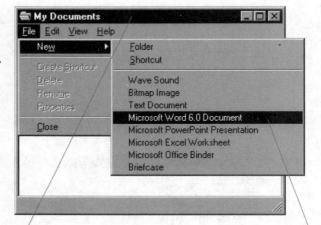

1 Open a folder (from My Computer or Windows Explorer) you want to create a file or folder in.

2 Click on File, move the mouse over New, and then click on Folder to create a new folder. To create a file click on one of the file formats in the bottom section of the menu.

3 Type a name for the file/folder created and then press the ENTER key.

Renaming a File/Folder

You can rename a file/folder at any time. It is done very easily too, by simply editing the current name.

 REMEMBER

Use the same method to rename icons on the desktop. You won't be able to rename the Recycle Bin though!

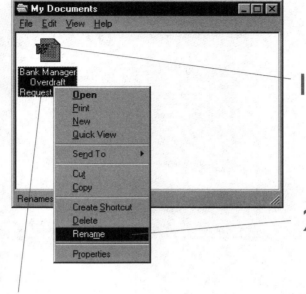

| Right-click on a file/folder to rename.

2 Click on Rename from the shortcut menu.

3 The current name will be boxed in heavier line. Type the new name, or use the cursor arrow keys to position the cursor and edit only part of the name.

4 Press the ENTER key or click your mouse pointer outside the file name to confirm the new name.

Backtracking File Operations

If you accidentally delete, rename, copy or move a file, you can undo the operation. Furthermore, you can now undo several preceding operations instead of just the last one (multilevel undo feature).

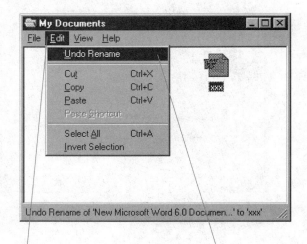

| | Click on Edit from any folder. At the top of the menu displayed, an Undo of the last file operation is displayed. | 2 | Click on the Undo operation. Repeat, if you need to undo any more operations. |

Finding Lost Files/Folders

The new Find feature in Windows 95 is very powerful and extensive. The search can be based on partial file names, date last modified, or text within the files. Once the desired files are found you can open them or perform other operations (including deleting, renaming, moving, displaying properties, etc.) – all from the search results displayed without going into Windows Explorer!

You can also search for files on other computers in your network.

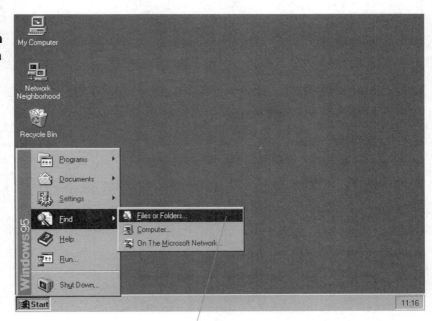

Point to Find from the Start button and click Files or Folders...

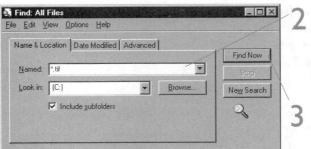

2 Click and then type in full/part name of the file or folder.

3 Click to start the search.

Creating Scraps

A 'scrap' is a piece of text copied/moved into a folder or onto the desktop, so that it can be used somewhere else by a simple drag operation. This technique serves the same purpose as the Cut, Copy and Paste operations described in Chapter 3, but it is more intuitive.

HANDY TIP **Keep the Shift key pressed when dragging the text block out to Move it instead of Copying.**

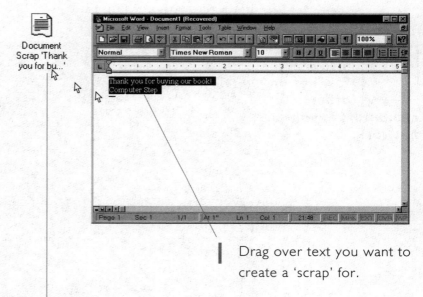

Drag over text you want to create a 'scrap' for.

2 Drag the block of text onto the desktop or folder.

HANDY TIP **Drag the Document Scrap icon onto the Recycle Bin icon to delete it, when no longer required.**

3 Drag the newly created Document Scrap into another document as required and its contents will be copied there.

Printing

Once you have created your document, you will usually want to obtain a hard copy of it, and so need to print it. This chapter shows you everything you need to know about printing.

Chapter Six

Covers

Printer Set Up

Before you set up your printer to work with Windows, ensure that it is connected to your computer and make a note of the printer manufacturer and model number.

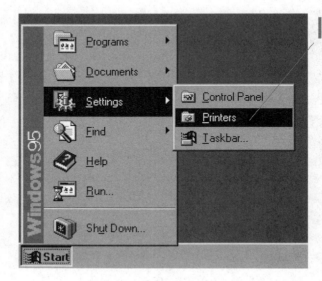

Click on the Start button, move pointer over Settings, and click Printers.

REMEMBER

A Network printer can be set up instead of a local one through the Add printer wizard.

2 Double-click the Add Printer icon.

3 Follow the instructions on screen given by the Add Printer wizard (see Chapter 1). An icon for your new printer is available in the Printers folder when finished.

Fonts

All the fonts installed on your computer are usually stored in one place: the Fonts folder (under the Windows folder in drive C).

You can manage these fonts easily by treating them as files. For example, you can add new fonts by dragging them to the Fonts folder, delete old ones by deleting them from the Fonts folder, etc... (see Chapter 5 for full details on all File operations).

Another useful feature now available is that you can preview any font before you decide to use it:

HANDY TIP

Change the View for further information about fonts. e.g. try the new, List Fonts by Similarity.

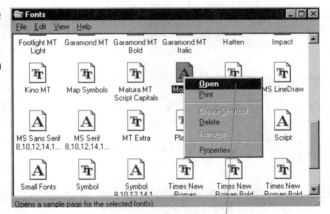

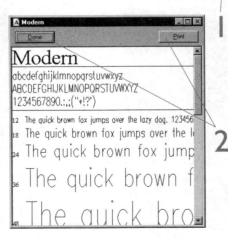

1 Right-click on the font you want to preview to display a shortcut menu and click on Open from it.

2 Preview of the selected font is displayed. Click on Print to get a printout of it, or just click Done.

Printing Documents

Once your printer is set up in Windows, printing is easy. You can print a document from the Program that created it or by dragging the file onto the Printer icon.

From the menu

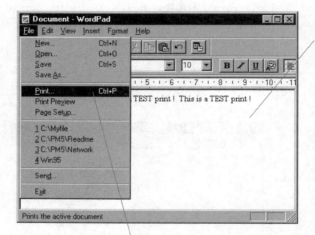

Type in some text in your application, or open a document you want to print.

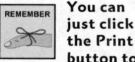

You can just click the Print button to print one copy of the whole document.

2 Click on File and then Print...

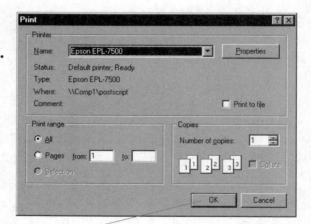

3 Click on OK after amending the options, if required (e.g. pages to print, no. of copies).

Using drag-and-drop

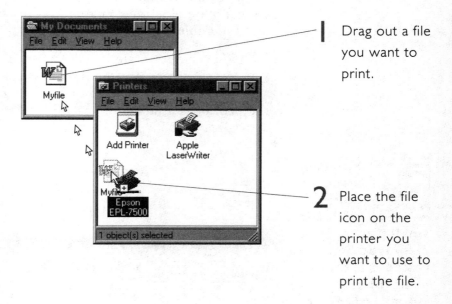

1 Drag out a file you want to print.

2 Place the file icon on the printer you want to use to print the file.

You can have a shortcut icon for a specific printer rather than the actual printer icon - if you are going to use the drag-and-drop technique often, create a shortcut icon for your main printer on the desktop (See Chapter 3).

Once you've dragged and dropped a file onto the printer icon, the program associated with the file is started and so is the printing – automatically!

Print Management

It is easy to find out which documents are currently printing and which are still waiting in the queue. Also shown is the document name, owner, size, when the print job was submitted.

Unlike previous versions, you can pause, resume or cancel your print jobs submitted on a network printer attached to another PC. There is no longer the need to walk to the PC the printer is attached to, as you had to in *Windows for Workgroups*.

 REMEMBER

You can also double-click the small printer icon displayed on the task bar after a print job is submitted (or right-click on it and select printer from the shortcut menu).

Epson
EPL-7500

Double-click on the printer icon your jobs are submitted to.

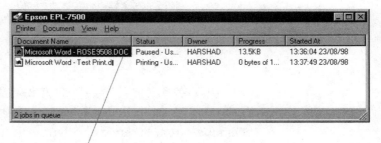

2 Click on the job you want to change the status of. Here Pause Printing from the Document menu was selected. This allows a job further down the queue to print before. Click on Pause Printing again to resume printing.

Note that whenever there is a problem, like paper jam, out-of-paper or just jobs paused, the small printer icon on the task bar has a red warning circle displayed. Move your mouse over it for an explanation, or click on it to display the print queue again - so that you can resume printing after

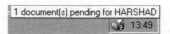

correcting any potential problems.

Configuration

You can configure many of your printer settings depending on the type of printer you have.

1   From the Printers folder, click once on the printer icon you want to configure. It will be highlighted.

2   Click on the File menu option, and then Properties.

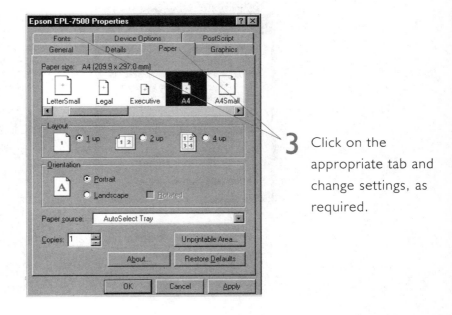

3   Click on the appropriate tab and change settings, as required.

Click on Print Test Page button (from the General tab) after you have first installed your printer to ensure that it works as expected. If it doesn't, Windows will guide you through so that the problem can be corrected.

Restore Defaults button is available from most tab settings so if you really make a mess of things, just click on this button.

Troubleshooting

Printing problems are common. If you experience difficulties, use the Windows Help system to resolve them.

1 Click on the Start button and then on Help.

2 Type "Print" in the Help Index and display the "Print Troubleshooting" entry from the list.

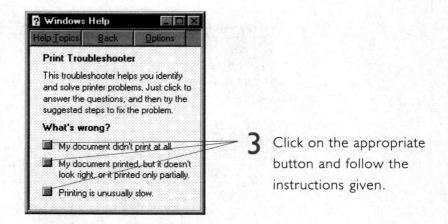

3 Click on the appropriate button and follow the instructions given.

Networking

Networking allows you to share information and resources between several computers linked together. You will be able to share files and printers with your colleagues at work and communicate with the world through the Internet.

Covers

Chapter Seven

Network Basics

A network is a group of computers linked together so that you can work more efficiently.

One of the main advantages of using a network is that there is no need to transfer information between computers using floppy disks. Instead, the information can stay where it is and you simply allow other users to share it, or other users allow you to share their information. This sharing of information can be extended to sharing of devices, like the printer or modem.

Since security may be an important consideration to you, it is possible to restrict access to information and resources by the use of passwords.

However, before you can use any of the networking features, you need to have the appropriate hardware installed. To network your computer to another, a special device, called *Network card* needs to be fitted. This controls the communication of your computer with another in the network (which also needs to have a network card). The computers are then physically connected, via the network cards, using special cables and connectors.

If you want to network your computer to remote sites, not possible by cabling, you need to have a *Modem* fitted. This device translates between computer and telephone signals. It can be fitted as a card you plug inside your computer (internal modem) or as a 'box' (external modem) you connect to the serial port (one of the sockets at the back of your computer). The modem is also connected to the telephone line.

Once you have a modem, you can communicate with the outside world. For example, you can have access to the Internet, send and receive E-Mail (electronic mail), transfer files to/from other computers, access your work computer from home (dial-up networking) and send faxes directly from your PC.

The Network Neighborhood

If the Network is already set up on your computer the Network Neighborhood icon appears on the desktop. From here, you can access shared resources on other computers.

Network
Neighborhood

1 Double-click on the Network Neighborhood icon.

REMEMBER

Your own computer appears here too.

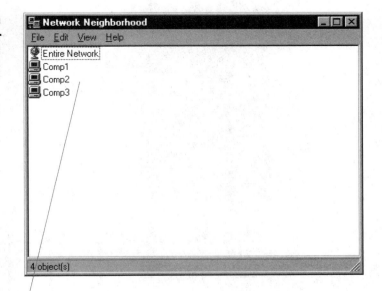

2 If there are computers connected to your workgroup, they'll appear here. Also, by double-clicking on the Entire Network icon, computers not in your workgroup will appear. Double-click on any computer to see what you can access from it.

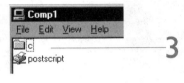

3 For example, from computer Comp1, you can access the whole of the C disk and the postscript printer connected to it.

Setting Up the Network Software

Before you can set up the software, the hardware must already be installed, as discussed.

If the Network Neighborhood icon appears on your desktop and Windows prompts you for a Network password when you switch on, the network is already set up on your computer.

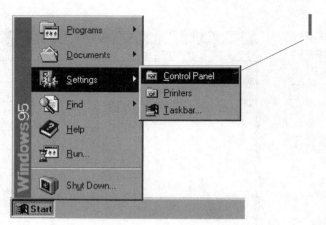

1 Click on the Start button, move over to Settings, and then click on Control Panel.

2 Double-click on the Network icon.

...cont'd

REMEMBER **Windows automatically sets up other necessary network components when you install the Adapter.**

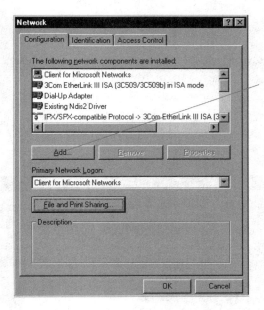

3 Click on Add... if your Adapter does not appear in the list displayed.

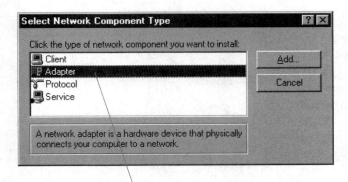

4 Click on Adapter to select it and then on the Add... button.

5 Follow the rest of the instructions, as given.

Naming your Computer on the Network

Once your Network software has been installed, you need to give your computer an identity on the network.

> Still from within the Network box, click the Identification tab at the top.

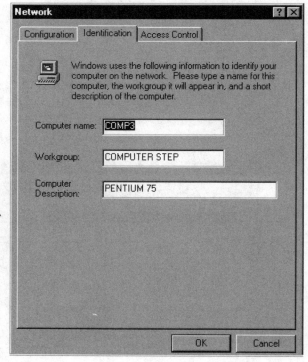

REMEMBER **The decription helps other users link to your computer.**

2 Type in your Computer name, Workgroup name, and a description of your computer. Then click OK.

Identifying a Network Device

If any device (printer, modem, disk drive, etc...) is a Network device rather than physically existing within your computer or attached to it, then the icon representing it has a small cable at the base, as shown here:

Epson
EPL-7500

This is a Network printer.

C on 'Comp1'   C on 'Comp2'
(E:)   (F:)

These are two Network disk drives from two different computers. They both give access to the whole C hard disk drive on Comp1 and Comp2 through logical drives E and F respectively. The cross on the second drive (F) indicates that it is not accessible at this time, probably because Comp2 has been switched off.

So you'll always know when you are using a Network device and whether it is accessible.

Sharing your Folders or Printers

To be able to share your files/documents you need to share the folder they are in. You can also share the printers attached to your computer with other users networked to your computer. Before you start though, click on the File and Print Sharing... button in the Network box to ensure that file and printer sharing is set up.

To share a folder

 HANDY TIP

To share an entire disk, right-click on a disk drive icon instead of a folder.

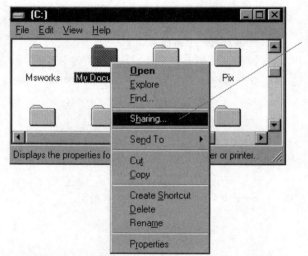

Right-click on the folder you want to share, and then click on the Sharing... option.

 REMEMBER

A little hand appears below the folder icon to indicate that it is shared.

My Documents

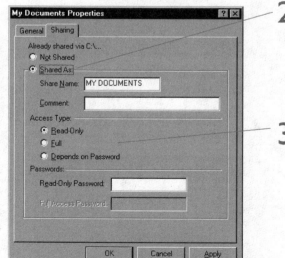

2 From the Sharing tab, click on the Shared As option.

3 Select Full if you allow others to update your files and type password(s), if appropriate.

To share your printer

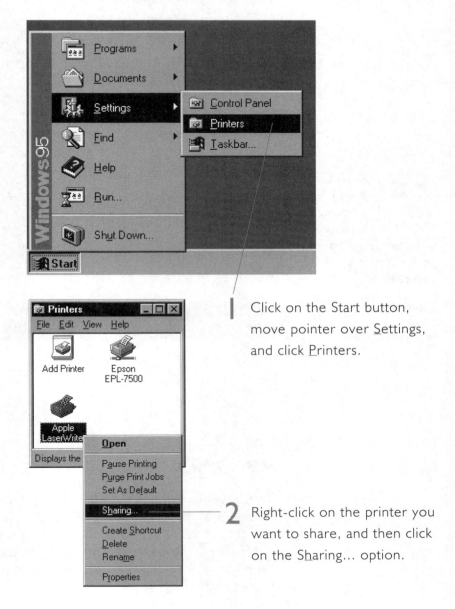

Click on the Start button, move pointer over Settings, and click Printers.

2 Right-click on the printer you want to share, and then click on the Sharing... option.

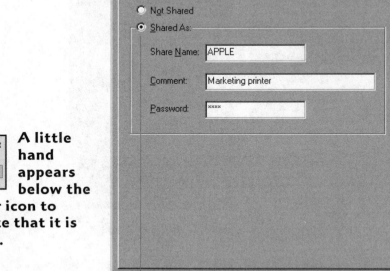

A little hand appears below the printer icon to indicate that it is shared.

Apple
LaserWriter

3 From the Sharing tab, click on the Shared As option. Then type a description to identify the printer and a password if you want to restrict access.

User-level access

So far we have looked at sharing of folders and printers by simply making them shareable and using a password perhaps to restrict access to certain people only. There is another way of giving permission to share your resources called *user-level access control*. In order to set this up follow these steps:

Click on the Start button, move over to Settings, and then click on Control Panel.

2 Double-click on the Network icon.

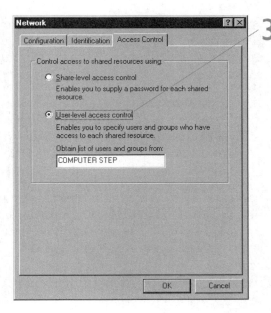

3 Click on the Access Control tab, and then on User-level access control option.

4 Now, when you select the Sharing... option for folders or printers, a list of names is displayed and you can decide access rights for each one.

Using Shared Resources from other Computers

Once a folder or a disk from another networked computer is shared (see previous topic), you can access it from your Network Neighborhood icon (see earlier topic). Simply open the folder from the other computer to use the files it contains.

If you are frequently going to use the same shared folder, then it is best to assign a logical drive letter to it (e.g. E, F, G, ...). Then, you can access it from My Computer or Windows Explorer in exactly the same way as any of your own physical drives.

Logical drives don't really exist - you are mapping, say a folder on the hard disk C in another computer to a logical drive E on your computer. You cannot map it as the same letter C because you already use it for your own hard disk drive. You can use several letters to map different folders from one or more other computers you are connected to.

From the Network Neighborhood or My Computer click on the Map Network Drive icon.

This is only available if the Toolbar option is on from the View menu.

REMEMBER

Click on Reconnect at logon option to ensure that this is automated when you log on (provided the computer in the path is on when you start yours).

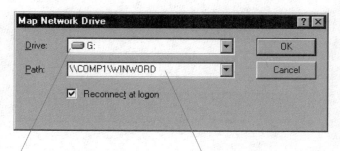

2 The next free drive letter appears here.

3 Type in the path for the folder (including the computer name).

...cont'd

Create a shortcut to a network resource, like a drive or printer, you use frequently (see Chapter 3 - Creating a Shortcut).

You can click the arrow on the right to choose a different drive letter than the next available one, or choose a path used previously rather than typing it in.

Right-click on the My Computer icon or the Network Neighborhood icon to display a shortcut menu, from which you can select the option Map Network Drive... instead of selecting it from the Toolbar icon inside the window. You can also select Disconnect Network Drive...from here or click on its icon next to the Map Network Drive icon from the Toolbar.

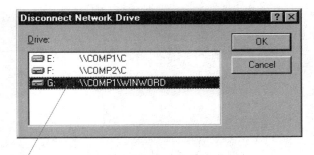

Click on the path you want to disconnect and then on OK.

Print a Test page before printing too many pages to ensure that the printer works as expected.

Before you can use a shared printer set up on another computer on the network, you will need to set it up again on your computer as a Network printer (See Chapter 6 on Printing). Then print your documents as normal using the new network printer.

Dial-Up Networking

This is particularly useful if you need to access your computer in the office from a computer in the home or from a portable computer if you are travelling.

A pre-requisite to using Dial-Up Networking is a modem installed at both ends (calling and server computers), access to a telephone line to dial in, and Dial-Up Networking set up on both computers. Then you can access any shared resource, like a folder or printer, directly from the server computer or from any other computer it is networked to.

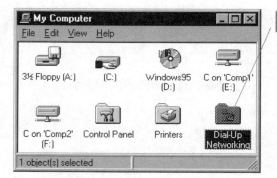

From My Computer double-click on Dial-Up Networking.

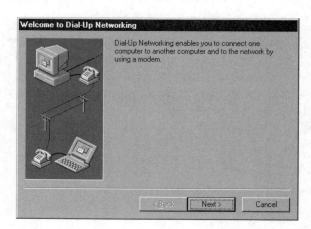

2 Follow the Wizard screens to set up Dial-Up Networking. These will vary depending on your particular set up.

Internet

The Internet is a term used to describe the global network of computers connected together predominantly using telephone lines. Various types of computers are linked to the Internet, ranging from the very small PC or laptop to large mainframe computers found in government departments and educational establishments.

Commercial companies, other organisations and private individuals are all using the Internet to send messages via E-Mail (electronic mail), to join news/discussion groups, to download useful files/programs, to browse at bulletin boards, and much more.

It is estimated that there are currently over 40 million people around the world using the Internet. However, this number will soon be out-of-date due to the phenomenal growth in the number of new connections every day.

Once you have a modem attached to your computer, Windows 95 provides a number of ways to become part of the Internet:

 or

The Microsoft Network

The Microsoft Network

The Microsoft Network (MSN). This is a new service available from Microsoft that you can subscribe to. Double-click on the MSN icon from the desktop.

Dial-Up Networking

Dial-Up Networking. Use this icon to connect to a service provider other than Microsoft.

You may of course already have Internet access through another service provider or prefer to sign-up with one, like AOL, CompuServe, Demon, Pipex, or from one of many others. They may have provided Internet access software for you to use, or recommended some that you can download from the Internet itself. There are some very good software utilities, including shareware, that will work under Windows 95.

Microsoft Internet Explorer

If you have bought and installed Microsoft Plus, an add-on package to Windows 95, you'll have, amongst other utilities, the Microsoft Internet Explorer. Alternatively, you can download the latest version of Internet Explorer from Microsoft's web site free-of-charge or obtain a CD copy from a magazine cover-mount.

This provides access to the Internet and the World Wide Web (WWW).

 You can download the latest version of Internet Explorer from – http://www. microsoft.com/ie

 or

The Internet   Internet Explorer

Double-click on The Internet icon from the desktop.

 Installing the latest version of Microsoft Internet Explorer also updates your Windows 95 – you'll have amongst other features, an Active Desktop and a Web-style view of Windows screens.

2 Type a valid address for a particular web site.

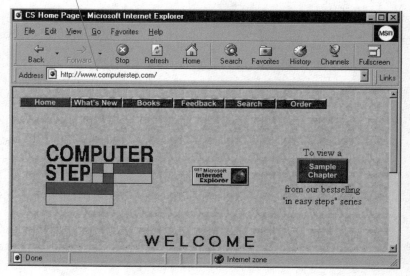

Customising

This chapter shows you how to change the way Windows looks on your computer and how to alter other settings to suit your needs.

Chapter Eight

Colours

You can change most of the colours you see in Windows and Windows applications to suit your taste. You can't however change the colours of the icons.

Right-click on any free space on the desktop. Then click on Properties from the short menu displayed.

Microsoft Plus, an add-on product, includes Desktop Themes you can choose from - these combine colours, wallpapers, mouse pointers, icons, sound events, etc. on specific concepts like Sports, Nature.

2 Click on the Appearance tab.

3 Click on this down-arrow then click on another colour Scheme from the list displayed. The preview for it is displayed on top.

At the bottom of the Color display table, click on Other... for a selection of further colours and to create custom colours.

4 Click on OK to confirm changes and close this window, or on Apply just to confirm the changes made.

You can change the colour of individual items instead of the whole scheme. Just click on the item from the preview (e.g. Inactive Window, Selected). Then alter the Size/Color by using the arrows next to these. If the item chosen includes text, you can change its font, size and colour in the same way.

Patterns and Wallpapers

You can change the desktop background with a pattern or a wallpaper of your choice. If you use a pattern and a wallpaper, the wallpaper will be displayed.

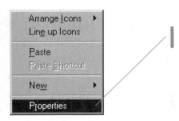

1 Right-click on any free space on the desktop. Then click on Properties from the short menu displayed.

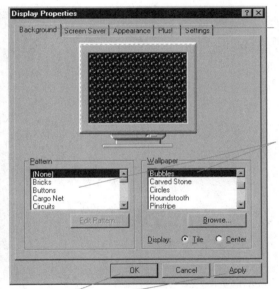

2 Click on the Background tab.

3 Click on a pattern or wallpaper you like, from the appropriate list.

REMEMBER **Centre displays a wallpaper once in the centre, Tile repeats it so that the whole desktop is filled.**

4 Click on OK to confirm changes and close this window, or on Apply just to confirm the changes made.

Click on the Edit Pattern... button to create your own patterns from the standard ones supplied. Click on the Browse... button to use a BMP file as a wallpaper - this can be any bit-mapped file that you can create using Paint or any other graphics program, or a scan of an image (like your company logo) saved as a bit-mapped file.

Screen Savers

Screen savers are images displayed on the screen when there is no activity for some time. This is supposed to prevent your screen from burn-out.

Right-click on any free space on the desktop. Then click on Properties from the short menu displayed.

2 Click on the Screen Saver tab.

3 Click on the pull-down arrow and select a Screen saver.

4 Click on up/down arrows to change the time of inactivity before the screen saver starts.

 Settings... allows you to vary the default variables of a screen saver (e.g. colours, speed) and depends on the screen saver.

5 Click on OK to confirm changes and close this window, or on Apply just to confirm the changes made.

Click on the Preview button to see the screen saver in action. To continue working after a screen saver display, press any key or move your mouse a little.

Date and Time

Your computer has an internal clock which can be reset at any time. It can be displayed on the taskbar at all times so that you always know what time it is while you are working.

 Date and Time is used by other programs and Windows itself.

To display the clock

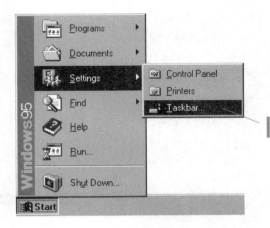

Click on the Start button, move your mouse pointer over Settings, and click on the Taskbar... option.

 You can also right-click on the taskbar and click on Properties from the shortcut menu to access this same window.

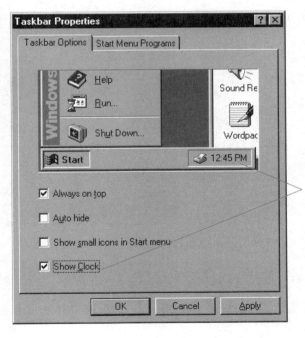

2 Click on the Show Clock option so that it's ticked and displayed on the taskbar preview.

...cont'd

To display the date

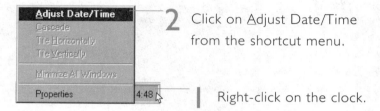 Move your mouse pointer over the time displayed on the taskbar and leave it there for a few seconds. The current date then pops up.

To reset date/time

2 Click on Adjust Date/Time from the shortcut menu.

| Right-click on the clock.

 Click on the Time Zone tab to change the Greenwich Mean Time for another country.

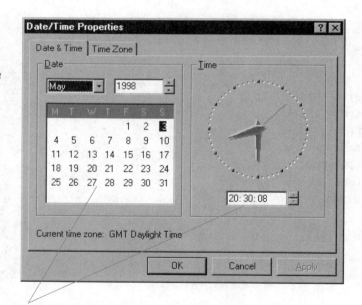

3 Click on another day (or change the month/year first above), or click inside the time box and either use the arrows or type the new time in the box.

Regional Settings

You can customise various country-specific settings. You may be running software that uses some of these settings and so if something isn't displayed as expected, then perhaps you need to change the regional settings.

Regional
Settings

Double-click on Regional Settings icon from the Control Panel window (Start menu, Settings).

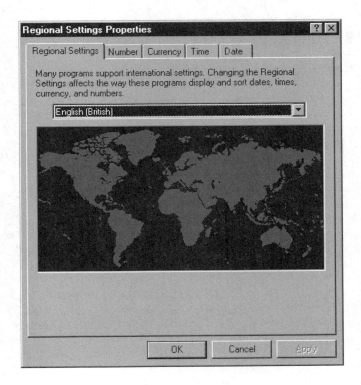

2 Click on the relevant tabs and change settings after selecting the language (nation) from the pull-down list.

Mouse

The make of mouse attached to your computer may be different from the Microsoft mouse shown here. However, similar customising options will still be offered.

Mouse

| Double-click on the Mouse icon from the Control Panel window (Start menu, Settings).

REMEMBER

Click on other tabs to change other settings for your mouse.

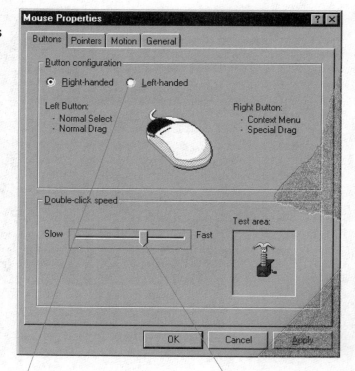

2 If you're left-handed, click on the Left-handed option.

3 Drag this slider to increase or decrease the speed at which a double-click on your mouse is recognised. Then test the double-click speed by double-clicking on the object in the Test area.

Keyboard

Like your mouse, your keyboard settings can be changed to suit your personal preference.

Keyboard

| Double-click on the Keyboard icon from the Control Panel window (Start menu, Settings).

REMEMBER

Click on other tabs to change other settings for your keyboard.

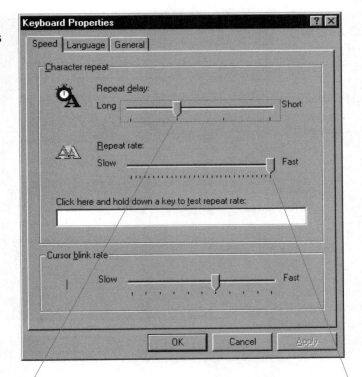

2 Drag the Repeat delay slider to set the time your computer waits before it starts repeating the first key when you have held it down.

3 Drag the Repeat rate slider to set how fast or slow a key repeats itself when you hold it down. Click in the test box and hold down a key to test the repeat rate.

Passwords

Your Windows password can be changed provided you can remember your current password.

Passwords

| Double-click on the Passwords icon from the Control Panel window (Start menu, Settings).

HANDY TIP

If more than one person is using the same PC, User Profiles will allow each to have their own customised desktop.

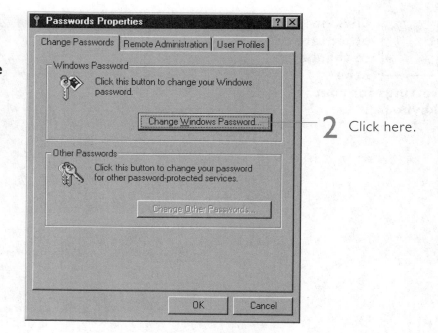

2 Click here.

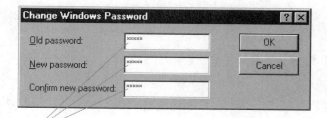

3 Type in your current password as Old, and your new password twice. Then click on OK.

Multimedia

Multimedia, as the name suggests, is the integration of several media formats including video and audio. Most new computers nowadays have a CD-ROM drive fitted and many also have a sound card and speakers.

Multimedia

Double-click on the Multimedia icon from the Control Panel window (Start menu, Settings).

REMEMBER **Use the multimedia programs available with Windows 95, like CD Player and Media Player, to play audio CDs and view animations.**

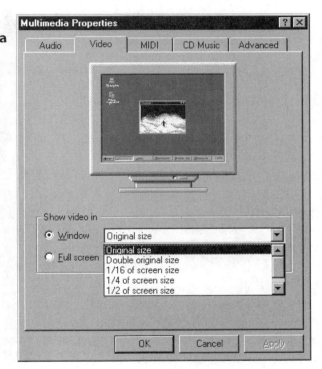

2 Click on the relevant tabs and change settings as required.

Sounds

You can assign different sounds to events that occur when using Windows, like when starting Windows, when you exit Windows, and so on. These will only work, of course, if you have a sound card fitted.

Sounds

I Double-click on the Sounds icon from the Control Panel window (Start menu, Settings).

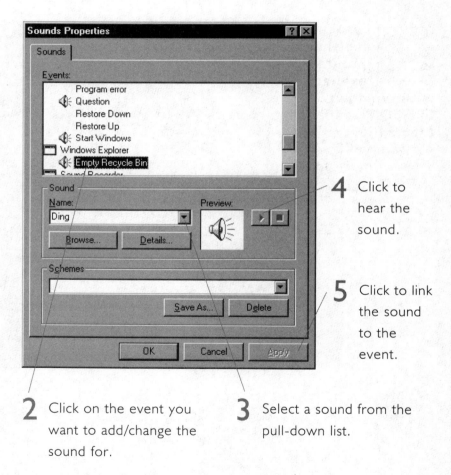

4 Click to hear the sound.

5 Click to link the sound to the event.

2 Click on the event you want to add/change the sound for.

3 Select a sound from the pull-down list.

Taskbar

The Taskbar, usually at the bottom of the screen, displays the Start button, clock, printer status, and task buttons for each open application.

To move/resize the Taskbar

1 Drag the taskbar (from a clear area) to the top, bottom, left or right edges.

HANDY TIP

Try not to have a large taskbar as it will reduce your desktop space.

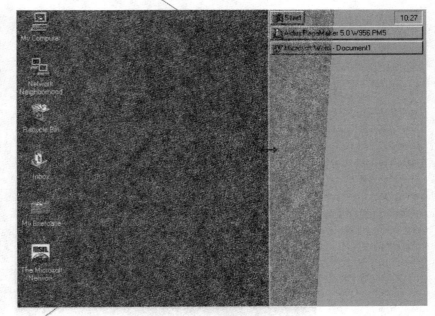

2 Move your mouse pointer over the inside edge of the taskbar so that it changes to a double-headed arrow. Then drag it in either direction to change the width of the taskbar.

...cont'd

To change Taskbar properties

Right-click on any free space on the taskbar and then click on Properties from the short menu displayed, or click on the Start menu, move the mouse over Settings and click on Taskbar...).

HANDY TIP

Select this to make the taskbar disappear, giving you more desktop space. You can still make it temporarily visible at any time by moving the mouse pointer over the relevant edge of the screen.

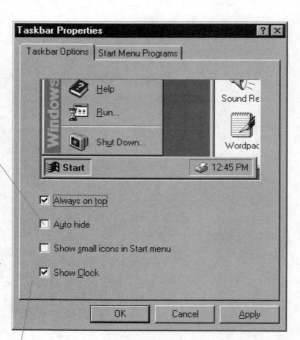

2 Click on the options required (so that they are ticked) or click on ticked options to turn off the feature and click OK.

Accessories

Accessories are basic programs and utilities provided with Windows. They might be adequate for some of your needs and you will not need to buy full-blown software packages offering similar functions. If a program described here is not available on your computer, install the relevant Windows component.

Chapter Nine

Covers

WordPad

Wordpad

WordPad is a basic word processor used to create and edit documents.

To start WordPad

1 Click on Start and move the mouse over Programs.

2 Move the mouse over Accessories.

3 Click on WordPad.

Creating a new document

To create a new document, simply start typing in WordPad

or

Click on New... from the File menu. This will allow you to choose the type of document to create (e.g. Word) although you can specify this when you save the document.

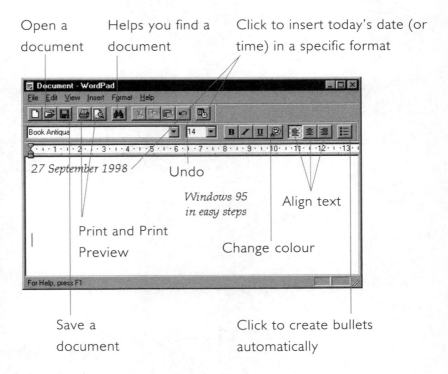

Open a document — Helps you find a document — Click to insert today's date (or time) in a specific format

27 September 1998 — Undo

Windows 95 in easy steps — Align text

Print and Print Preview — Change colour

Save a document — Click to create bullets automatically

Editing

1 Move the mouse pointer to the start of the text you want to edit - it will change to an I-beam. Then click on the mouse and drag it to the end of the text-string you want to edit. The selected piece of text will be highlighted.

2 Press the Del key on your keyboard to delete the selected text, or type in some new text to replace it.

3 Drag the selected text to another part of the text block to move it, or press the Control key when dragging to make a copy of it elsewhere.

Paint

Mspaint

Paint is a basic drawing and painting program. It can also be used to enhance images scanned using a scanner.

| Click on Start and move the mouse over Programs, then Accessories, and then click on Paint.

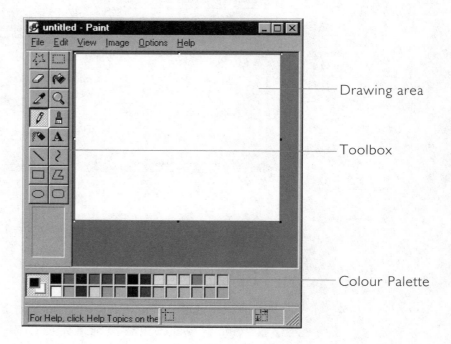

Drawing area

Toolbox

Colour Palette

Toolbox

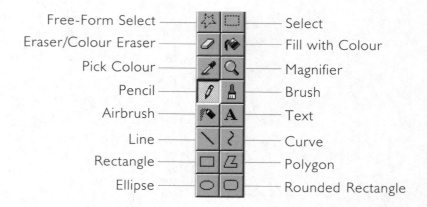

Free-Form Select	Select
Eraser/Colour Eraser	Fill with Colour
Pick Colour	Magnifier
Pencil	Brush
Airbrush	Text
Line	Curve
Rectangle	Polygon
Ellipse	Rounded Rectangle

...cont'd

Drawing

If you make a mistake, click on Image from the menu and then Clear Image - then start all over again.

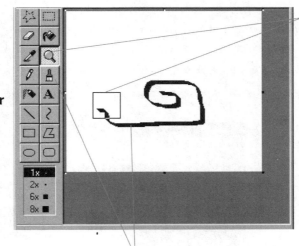

2 Click on the magnifier - a rectangular box will appear in the drawing area.

3 Click on a section to zoom in 8x.

1 Click on a tool to draw with (brush used here) and drag the mouse in the drawing area.

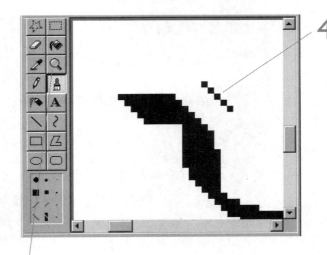

4 Edit drawing - left mouse button adds pixels in the foreground colour and the right button in background colour.

5 Zoom out to normal 1x magnification when finished.

6 Save the file (File, Save As...).

Phone Dialer

Dialer

This is a useful program, especially if you don't have a speed dial facility on your phone. Before you can use it though, you'll need a modem connected to your computer and it must be the type you can connect your phone into.

| Click on Start and move the mouse over Programs, then Accessories, and then click on Phone Dialer.

Click on the drop-down list to access previously dialled numbers.

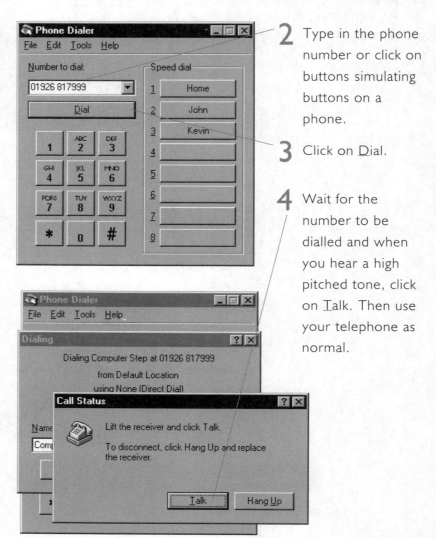

2 Type in the phone number or click on buttons simulating buttons on a phone.

3 Click on Dial.

4 Wait for the number to be dialled and when you hear a high pitched tone, click on Talk. Then use your telephone as normal.

Speed dialling

| Click on one of the empty Speed dial buttons to program it.

To change or delete a Speed dial number, click on the **Edit** menu and then **Speed Dial...**

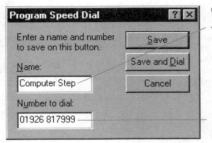

2 Type a name associated with the number you want to see on the Speed dial button.

3 Type the telephone number.

Standard settings

| Click on Tools and then Dialing Properties...

Click here to select a calling card to use, like British Telecom, Mercury, **and to enter it so that it's always used when you make a call.**

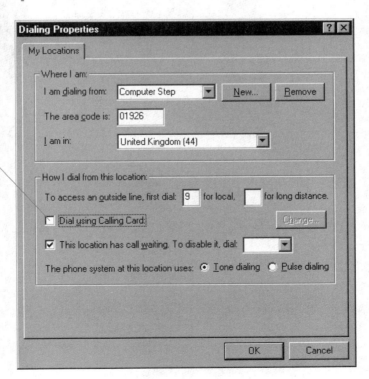

Media Browser

Mbrowser

Media Browser lets you play/view video, sound and pictures stored as collections on CD-ROM discs.

| Click on Start and move the mouse over Programs, then Accessories, and then click on Media Browser.

HANDY TIP **You can even add your own collection** of graphics, presentations or spreadsheets from the hard disk.

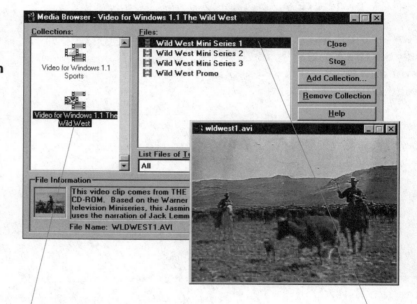

2 Double-click on a collection that's been added.

3 Double-click on a file to play/view.

The Add Collection... button allows you to add collections from your CD or hard disk.

Character Map

Charmap

The Character Map enables you to use characters and special symbols from other character sets in your document.

1 Click on Start and move the mouse over <u>P</u>rograms, then Accessories, and then click on Character Map.

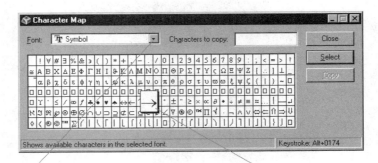

2 Click and select the font from the drop-down list.

3 Click and hold down the mouse to magnify the character.

4 Double-click on a character to copy it to the clipboard – from here you can paste it into your document. Alternatively, look at the keystroke (bottom right) for the character and use that to generate the character in your document.

If you need to copy several characters to your document, click on a character and then on the <u>S</u>elect button. Once the string of characters is built up, in sequence, in the Characters to Copy box (top right), click on the <u>C</u>opy button to copy them all to the clipboard.

Calculator

Calc

The Calculator provides both Standard and Scientific calculators.

1 Click on Start and move the mouse over Programs, then Accessories, and then click on Calculator.

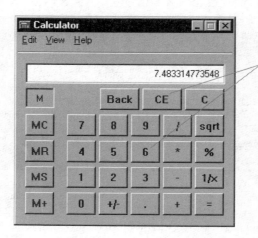

2 Click on the relevant buttons (similar to buttons on a hand-held calculator) or type the values from the keyboard.

3 To perform trigonometric and statistical functions, click on the View menu and then Scientific.

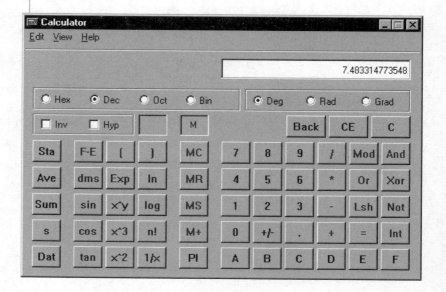

Cardfile

Cardfile

Cardfile lets you store the type of information kept on a manual card index. Examples include Names, Addresses and Phone numbers.

I   Click on Start and move the mouse over Programs, then Accessories, and then click on Cardfile.

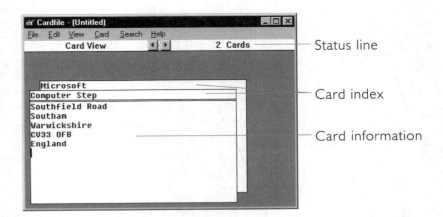

— Status line

— Card index

— Card information

2   To create new cards, click on New from the File menu and type the details in the Card information area. e.g. Address.

3   Double-click on the Card index line to display an index dialog box. Type in the index for the card. e.g. Name.

HANDY TIP

Click on List from the View menu to display just the index of all cards alphabetically.

4   To create more cards, click on Add from the Card menu. The Add dialog box is displayed. Type the Card index here and click on OK. Then the card is displayed and you can type the main details in the Card information area.

5   Click on the Forward or the Backward arrow in the Status line to look through information in a set of cards.

Clipboard Viewer

Clipbrd

A Clipboard is a temporary storage area. It is used to transfer information (text and graphics) between applications and within the same document.

Whenever you select an object/text from an application and click on Cut or Copy from the Edit menu, it goes into the Clipboard. The Print Screen button on your keyboard also copies the whole screen to the clipboard and Alt+Print Screen button copies just the active window to the clipboard. To copy the contents of the clipboard somewhere else later on, click on Paste from the Edit menu. See Cut, Copy and Paste in Chapter 3, Working with Programs.

It is not necessary to use Clipboard Viewer to perform the Cut, Copy and Paste functions. However, you must remember that the contents of the clipboard are overwritten if you copy something else in it and cleared when you quit Windows. Therefore the main benefit of using Clipboard Viewer is to save its contents and for subsequent retrieval.

1 Click on Start and move the mouse over Programs, then Accessories, and then click on Clipboard Viewer.

HANDY TIP

Press the Del key to clear the contents of the clipboard.

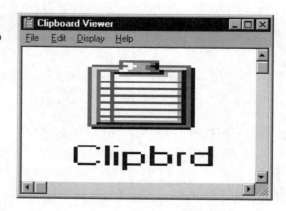

2 Click on File, Save As... to save the current contents of the clipboard as a .clp file.

Disk Tools

Windows 95 includes a set of tools or programs to prepare your disks for use and to keep them working efficiently. You'll also be able to secure the information stored on them, away from the computer for peace of mind.

Chapter Ten

Covers

Disk Properties

As for other objects in Windows 95, you can easily access the Properties dialog box for a disk. Then, you can check general details about your disk, like the amount of free space available, and perform *housekeeping* routines like Defragment the disk, Backup, etc.

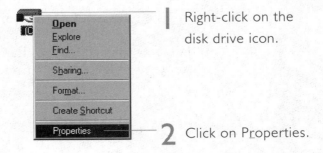

I Right-click on the disk drive icon.

2 Click on Properties.

Click on the Sharing tab to share your whole disk on the network - See Chapter 7.

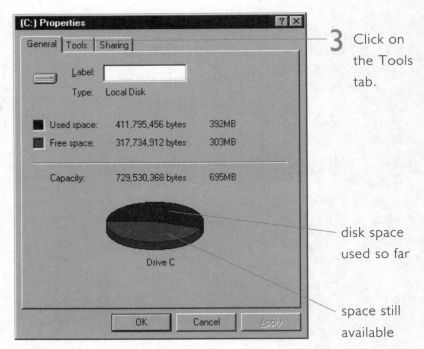

3 Click on the Tools tab.

disk space used so far

space still available

...cont'd

REMEMBER

The same Tools are available from the Start button, Programs, Accessories, System Tools.

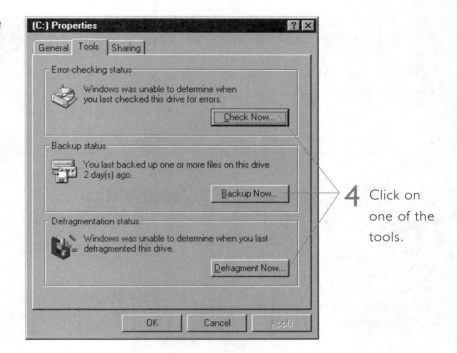

4 Click on one of the tools.

HANDY TIP

System Agent, available only from the Microsoft Plus add-on, allows you to automatically schedule some of these routines at specific dates and times.

Check Now...   looks for disk errors and fixes them. See ScanDisk (later in this chapter).

Backup Now...   allows you to make secure copies of your data. See Backup (later in this chapter).

Defragment Now...   reorganises the disk to speed up file access. See Disk Defragmenter (later in this chapter).

Formatting Floppy Disks

Most floppy disks are pre-formatted, for ease of use.

Before you can use floppy disks to copy or store files on you may have to prepare them for use with the Format option.

1 Insert a new floppy disk, or one you need to overwrite, into the floppy disk drive.

2 Open My Computer or Windows Explorer.

It's often useful to reformat (overwrite) disks. However, make sure you're not overwriting data you need!

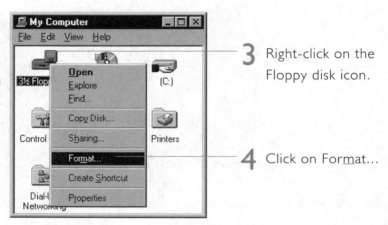

3 Right-click on the Floppy disk icon.

4 Click on Format...

Although a label is optional, type in something meaningful (up to 11 characters) to easily identify the disk in future.

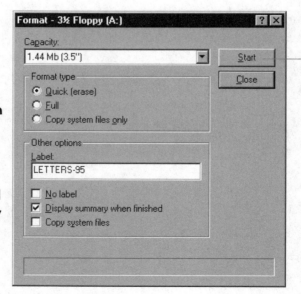

5 Select options and click on Start.

Files are stored on a disk in *allocation units*, so say an allocation unit is 512 bytes (this is same as 512 characters or 0.5K), then a small file will occupy just one allocation unit and a larger file may occupy several allocation units.

The number and size of allocation units on a disk determines its storage capacity. The Format option will automatically allocate the right number of these, depending on the storage capacity of your floppy disk and the type of disk drive you have. Most just use 3.5" high density format (1.44MB) disks as standard.

You can do a quick Format in a fraction of the time if the floppy disk has been formatted once before. This is useful for reusing floppies with files that are no longer required.

Another option offered is to copy system files onto floppy disks so that if your main hard disk is corrupted to such an extent that you cannot even start your computer, then at least you can start it from a backup of the main system files held on a floppy disk.

After formatting has been completed successfully, basic information is displayed in a dialog box.

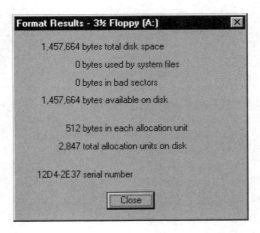

ScanDisk

ScanDisk allows you to analyse and repair problems with your disk. Although it is common to use it on your hard disk (even though it may be compressed using DriveSpace – see later), you can use it on floppy disks too.

| Click on ScanDisk from Start button, Programs, Accessories, System Tools (or similar if you have rearranged your Start menu programs), or run it from Disk Properties.

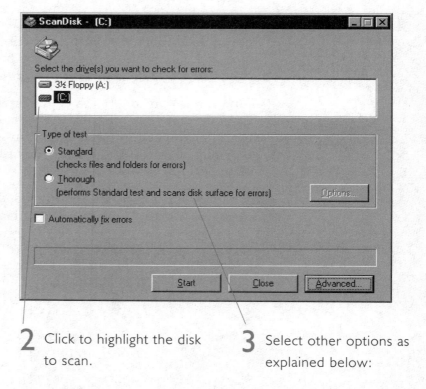

2 Click to highlight the disk to scan.

3 Select other options as explained below:

The Standard test will perform basic checks like, look for *Lost file fragments* – over time files can become fragmented on a disk (see Disk Defragmenter for more details), and so different parts are linked together by pointers. If these pointers are corrupted, then some parts of a file cannot be retrieved. ScanDisk can find these fragments and either delete them from the disk to free up space or create special files to write them into. The files created are called CHKDSK.001, CHKDSK.002, and so on. You can try and recover the fragments lost from these files, but more often than not you will not be successful.

Another standard check is for *Cross-linked files*. This is when there are two pointers addressing the same file block. Pointers have to be unique so this condition is an error. It is worth opting to Make copies of the file block that has two pointers in the hope that at least one of the files can be rescued. Select this and other options from the Advanced... button and the subsequent dialog box.

The default options shown are recommended.

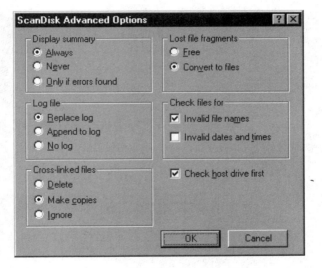

Although a Thorough scan takes longer, it is worth running it frequently on your important disk.

The Thorough scan option performs a disk surface scan too. This reads and writes back each *cluster* (or allocation unit) on disk to ensure that there are no problems. If the disk had been compressed by DriveSpace (see later), it will also check that data can be decompressed from it.

The surface scan can fix errors by trying to write data from *bad sectors* found on disk to another area on the disk.

Disk Defragmenter

A file is not always stored in a single contiguous disk location. It may be split and stored in different areas of the disk, particularly if you are frequently updating and deleting your files. This fragmentation doesn't damage the files, but when you want to access them, it takes longer. This is because first of all, at the end of each file fragment, a pointer needs to be read to give the address of where the next fragment is stored on disk. Then, the disk heads may need to move to an entirely different part of the disk to retrieve the chained fragment. This process can continue depending on how fragmented a particular file has become, making the access inefficient and slow.

You can reorganise your disk so that each file stored (perhaps as several pieces scattered all over the disk) is read and then written back in continuous storage locations. This will speed up access to all your files when you need to use them again.

| Click on Disk Defragmenter from Start button, Programs, Accessories, System Tools (or similar if you have rearranged your Start menu programs), or run it from Disk Properties.

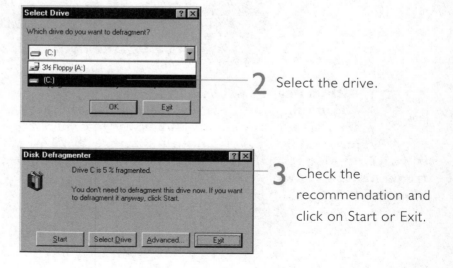

2 Select the drive.

3 Check the recommendation and click on Start or Exit.

...cont'd

4 Click to see
Defragmenter
working.

Your main hard disk drive will take about half an hour to defragment, depending on how fragmented it is, the size of the disk, and the speed of your computer.

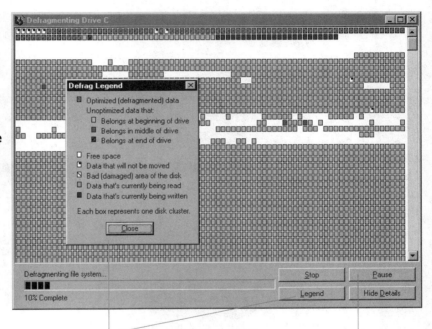

Click on the Legend button to see what the different coloured squares are.

Click to temporarily pause the defragmenting. This will speed up other Windows programs you may be running at the same time.

DriveSpace

DriveSpace prepares your disk drive so that all the files you store are compressed. This effectively has the effect of roughly doubling your disk capacity. Although it is common to install DriveSpace on your hard disk, you can also install it on floppy disks, especially if you're using them for backups.

> Click on DriveSpace from Start button, Programs, Accessories, System Tools (or similar if you have rearranged your Start menu programs).

HANDY TIP

Compressing your main C drive can take a long time, so schedule this task at the end of a day or a quiet period.

2 Select the drive to compress.

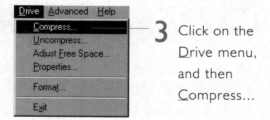

3 Click on the Drive menu, and then Compress...

DriveSpace can only compress up to 256MB of uncompressed disk space into a maximum of 512MB of compressed disk space. If your hard disk is larger than this, DriveSpace can create a second drive for all the uncompressed space. It needs to create this new second host drive anyway to move some system files into because they cannot be compressed.

DriveSpace 3

If you have installed the Microsoft Plus add-on package to Windows 95, you will automatically run DriveSpace 3. This has no limitation on how much disk space it can compress. The compression is also much tighter than using just DriveSpace, so you effectively get much more disk space.

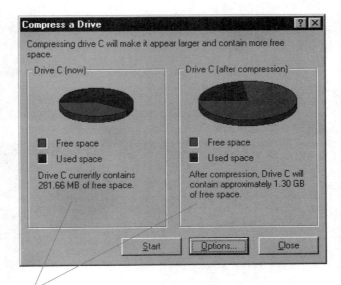

4 Compare the benefit of compressing your drive and click on Start if you are going to gain substantial Free space.

 Although rare, some files may become corrupted when DriveSpace is running - take the advice of doing a Back Up first.

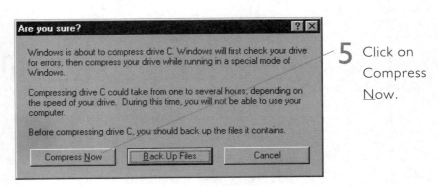

5 Click on Compress Now.

Backup

Hard disk drives have a life-span which averages around five years, although it will vary from make to make. Eventually, any hard disk drive will fail and when it does, anything stored on it is likely to be lost. Obviously, this is a very serious problem.

To safeguard yourself against this problem, you should take regular backups from your hard disk. A backup is a copy of files from your hard disk to another storage medium like floppy disks, Iomega Jaz cartridge or a tape storage device.

1 Click on Backup from Start button, Programs, Accessories, System Tools (or similar if you have rearranged your Start menu programs), or run it from Disk Properties.

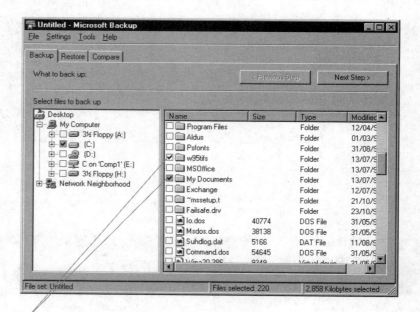

2 From a display (similar to Windows Explorer), select files or folders to backup. Click on the little box in front of a file/folder to select it for backup, so that a tick ☑ appears inside. If only some files are selected from a folder the tick-box appears shaded ☑. To deselect, click again.

...cont'd

3 Once all the files/folders are selected for this backup, click on the Next Step> button.

HANDY TIP

If you regularly backup the same set of files, click on Save As... from the File menu to save your selection. Then next time just load it in from File, Open File Set...

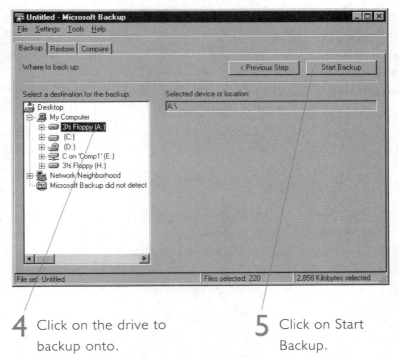

4 Click on the drive to backup onto.

5 Click on Start Backup.

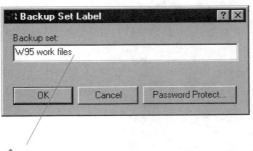

6 Type in a meaningful name for the backup set.

...cont'd

 If your backup does not fit onto one floppy disk, feed in new floppies when prompted and number them sequentially.

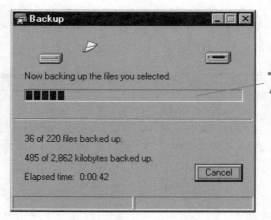

7 Monitor the progress. Insert new backup disks when prompted.

Comparing backed up files

If you want to check that the backup has worked properly, use the Compare tab. Select the files in the same way as you did for Backup.

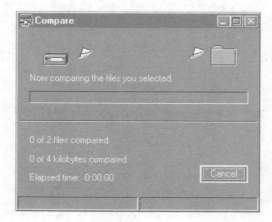

The animation brings two files from the two sources together in mid-air and ticks them when they join to indicate that they match.

Restore

After you have made a backup you may, at a future date, need to restore the backed up files to your hard disk. You can choose to restore the whole set of files exactly as backed up, or just a selection of files from the backup set.

I From the Backup window, click on the Restore tab.

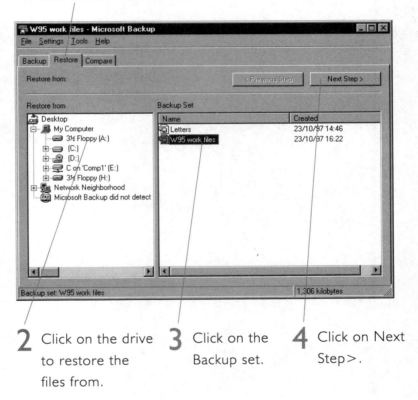

2 Click on the drive to restore the files from.

3 Click on the Backup set.

4 Click on Next Step>.

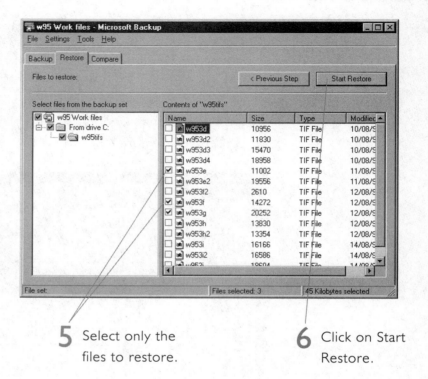

5 Select only the
files to restore.

6 Click on Start
Restore.

Microsoft Exchange

Microsoft Exchange enables you to send and receive messages (Mail) within your local network, or to the outside world through E-Mail if you have an Internet connection (including the Microsoft Network). If you have a faxmodem installed you can even exchange faxes.

Alternatively, if you have a newer version of Windows/use the MSN online service/installed the latest version of Microsoft Internet Explorer, then you'll have Microsoft Outlook Express instead. Refer to the relevant "in easy steps" title for this component.

Covers

Chapter Eleven

Installing Microsoft Exchange

If you didn't install Microsoft Exchange when you first installed Windows 95, you only need to install this component. If the Inbox icon doesn't appear on your desktop then Microsoft Exchange probably isn't installed.

1 Click on Start and move the mouse over Settings, then click on Control Panel.

2 Double-click on Add/Remove Programs.

You can install Microsoft Fax from here too (if you intend to use this and have a faxmodem).

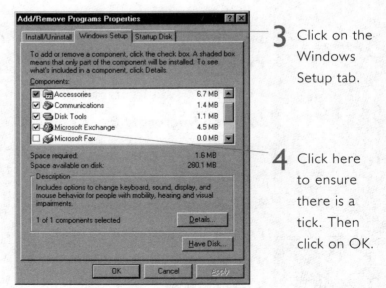

3 Click on the Windows Setup tab.

4 Click here to ensure there is a tick. Then click on OK.

5 Wizards will then guide you to configure Microsoft Exchange.

Choosing Services

Microsoft Exchange allows you to exchange messages in several ways (Internet, faxes, local mail, etc.). You can alter the basic services offered after they are first set up through the Microsoft Exchange installation wizard.

Double-click on the Mail and Fax icon from the Control Panel.

HANDY TIP

Initially services are stored in a default profile called, MS Exchange Settings. You can create other profiles for other users and set up different services in them.

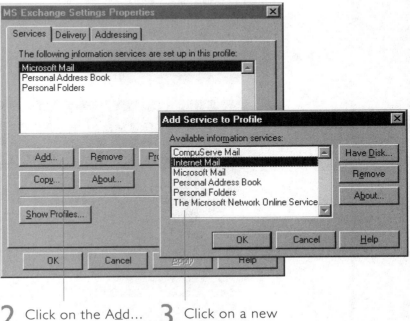

2 Click on the Add... button.

3 Click on a new service and OK.

Postoffice Administration

If you have set up the Microsoft Mail service (which allows you to send and receive Mail from your colleagues in your local area network or workgroup), you will need to set up a Postoffice for the management of mail on one of the computers. Other computers on the network just need to be told where the Postoffice is and need full (write) access to the folder on the computer it resides.

The Microsoft Exchange installation wizard will guide you in setting up/using the Postoffice for Microsoft Mail. If you are nominated the Postoffice Administrator then it should be set up on your machine and you will have the task of adding and removing Mail users. As the Administrator you will have the ultimate control of who uses Microsoft Mail.

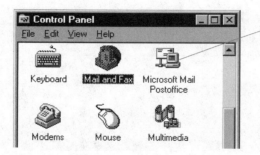

Double-click on the Microsoft Mail Postoffice icon from the Control Panel.

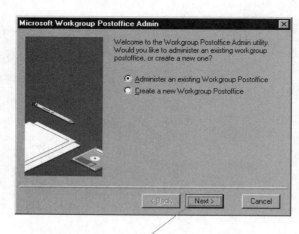

2 Follow the Postoffice Admin Wizard.

...cont'd

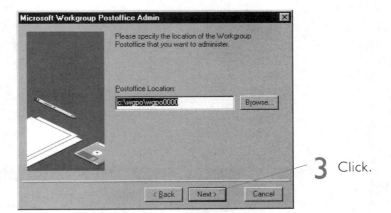

3 Click.

BEWARE

If you, as the admin-istrator forget your password, you will have to delete the main Postoffice folder (wgpo) and start again.

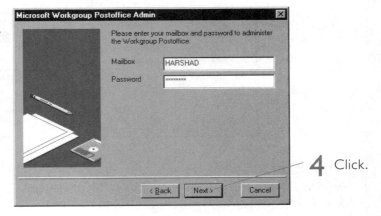

4 Click.

REMEMBER

The default password is called PASSWORD.

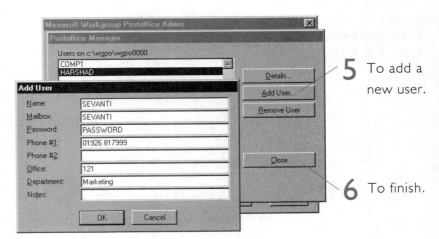

5 To add a new user.

6 To finish.

Starting Microsoft Exchange

Inbox

| Double-click on the Inbox icon from the desktop, or select Microsoft Exchange from Programs after clicking on the Start button.

The Microsoft Exchange window is similar to Windows Explorer – the left pane displays folders and the right displays the contents of a selected folder.

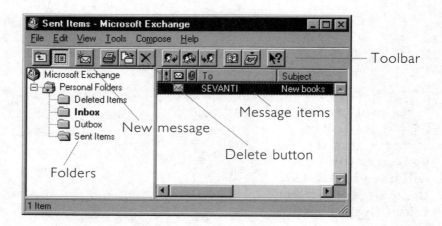

Other folders can be set up for specific projects – click on New Folder... from the File menu.

Deleted Items — transfers deleted messages here when you select messages and click on the Delete button on the toolbar. Select and Delete them again from here to permanently delete them.

Inbox — stores incoming messages. Highlighted if it contains Unread messages.

Outbox — your messages waiting to be sent.

Sent Items — stores messages you have sent.

Message item prefixes

important message ———— file attached with message

message type – mail, fax, etc.

Checking your Mail

Your outgoing mail is sent at the same time as incoming mail is delivered.

You can use the Microsoft Exchange window to:

- check for mail (see below)

- read your mail

- reply to mail

- forward on mail

- send new mail

Click on <u>T</u>ools.

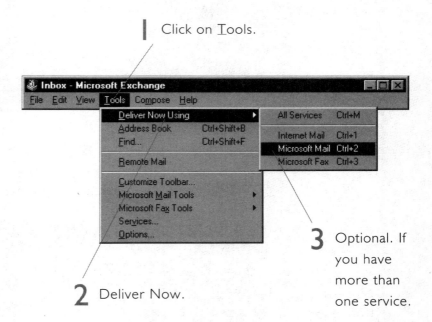

2 Deliver Now.

3 Optional. If you have more than one service.

See pages 152-154 for how to read/send mail.

Reading a Message

 Unread message items are bold.

Click on Inbox.

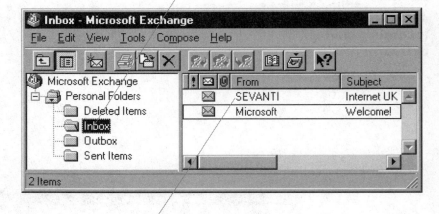

2 Double-click on message item.

displays next message

 Here, the message selected in step 2 is displayed.

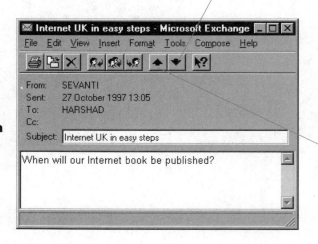

displays previous message

Replying to a Message

| Open a message window (see Reading a Message).

 2 Click on the Reply to Sender button from the toolbar.

4 Click on the
Send button.

 Click on these buttons as required:

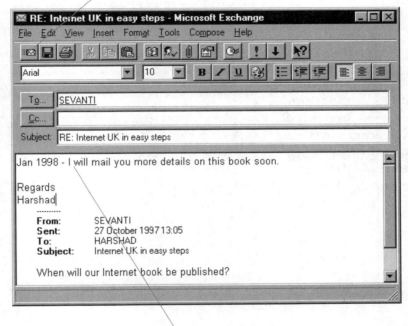

attach a file to message

request a Read receipt so you will know when the message was read

flag the message high Importance.

3 Type your reply here.

 Click on the Reply to All button instead to send the reply to all the recipients of the message you were reading.

Forwarding a Message

1 Open a window containing a message you want to forward.

 2 Click on the Forward button from the message window.

 **Here, the sample message provided with Microsoft Exchange is being forwarded on to someone else.**

3 In the Forward window (see above) click on the To... button and select a name from the Address book (see Composing a New Message).

4 Follow steps 3 and 4 on page 153.

Composing a New Message

1 Click on the New Message button in the Exchange window (or choose it from the Compose menu).

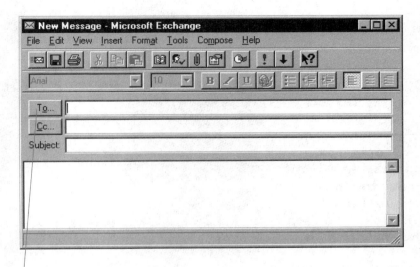

2 Type the name of the recipient and click the Check Names button or Click on the To... button to select the name from the Address book.

New... allows you to add names to your own Personal Address Book and also create your own Personal Distribution List so a group of people can receive your message when you send it to one name.

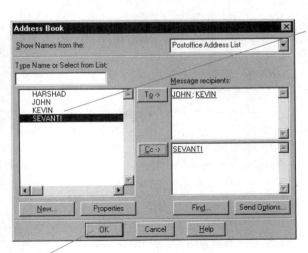

3 Select name and click on To & Cc (courtesy copy) buttons. Add as many names as you want.

4 Click OK and follow steps 3, 4 from Replying to a Message.

Faxing

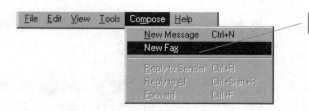

1 Click on New Fax option from the Compose menu.

You can fax any mail message – Use **T**ools, **F**ax Addressing Wizard to put the fax number into the **T**o... box – then send the mail to fax it.

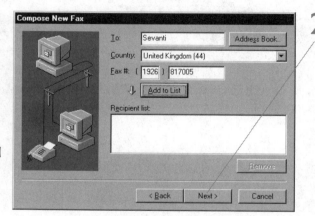

2 Wizards will guide you from selecting a recipient from the Address Book and choosing a cover page, to sending the fax.

Faxes sent are stored in the Sent Items folder.

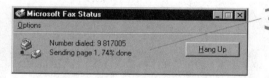

3 The Microsoft Fax Status window will pop up displaying the progress and any problems.

Viewing incoming faxes

In the Inbox folder, if a message item has "Fax from.." under the Subject column, double-click on it to automatically start the Fax Viewer.

Fax Viewer allows you to see the fax on screen, and includes features like zooming, rotating and displaying all the pages in a multipage fax. You can also obtain a paper-copy by printing the fax from the Fax Viewer window.

Index